The Character of the True Christian

A Study of the Beatitudes

PAULO JUNIOR

 Press

The Character of the True Christian: A Study of the Beatitudes
Copyright © 2024 by Paulo Junior.

Published by G3 Press
4979 GA-5
Douglasville, GA 30135
www.G3Min.org

All rights reserved. No part of this publication may be reproduced, stored in a retrieval system, or transmitted in any form by any means, electronic, mechanical, photocopy, recording, or otherwise, without prior permission of the publisher, except as provided for by USA copyright law.

Printed in the United States of America by Graphic Response, Atlanta, GA.

ISBN: 978-1-959908-21-0

I dedicate this book to my wife, Susana, who, like no other, has understood and has carried with me the burden of the Christian ministry

Contents

Foreword 1

Introduction 9

Chapter 1 – The Sermon on the Mount 13

Chapter 2 – The Beatitudes 39

Chapter 3 – Blessed Are the Poor in Spirit 55

Chapter 4 – Blessed Are Those Who Mourn.. 67

Chapter 5 – Blessed Are the Meek 83

Chapter 6 – Blessed are Those Who Desire Righteousness 99

Chapter 7 – Blessed Are the Merciful 127

Chapter 8 – Blessed Are the Pure in Heart 151

Chapter 9 – Blessed Are the Peacemakers... 177

Chapter 10 – Blessed Are the Persecuted.. 193

Conclusion – A Word to the Blessed... 215

Foreword

Joel R. Beeke

God is the happiest of all Beings. In His glorious perfections and in the love between the persons of the Trinity, He enjoys timeless, ineffable, and unending happiness. Through the gospel of Jesus Christ, this triune God invites us into the bliss of communion with Himself. Those in whom His Spirit works regeneration look far different than what the world considers to be a happy man or woman, for they are poor, they mourn, they are meek, and they are hungry and thirsty; but it is *they*—and *only* they—says Jesus, who are truly rich, happy, strong, and satisfied. True happiness, you see, is only found in union with God, the One who is in eternal joy and has come to us in the incarnate Word, the Lord Jesus Christ.

My dear friend, are *you* truly happy, tasting blessedness, fulfillment, and satisfaction in a heart full of joy? Our world is broken, dark, and often miserable. In the twenty-first century, we are far richer and more connected than any generation that has preceded us in history—but our society is more miserable than ever before. The true happiness that Christ provides through the gospel, however, is like a lighthouse shining through the darkness or like salt that seasons and preserves food (Matt. 5:13).

Everyone is on the quest for peace and happiness, but most people are using the wrong map. Many use maps that promise satisfaction through wealth, power, pleasure, fame, or security. Which is *your* map to happiness? From where are *you* seeking happiness? Every attempt to find happiness outside God is but a broken cistern, for it is only the triune God—the fountain of living waters—who can satisfy hungry and thirsty souls (Jer. 2:13; John 4:14; 7:37). Sin is a hard taskmaster that promises much but delivers little. The Beatitudes are an oasis in a desert for those who are sin-sick and convicted by the Holy Spirit. The gospel of Jesus Christ is sweet for such sin-sick people—those who the Holy Spirit has awakened to their guilt, shame, and unhappiness. This is precisely why even tax collectors and prostitutes fled to Jesus (Mark 2:16).

The Beatitudes are a map of sorts, but totally unlike the misleading maps of this world, for the Beatitudes are the divinely revealed map given by the Prince of Peace and Wonderful Counsellor foretold by the prophet Isaiah (Isa. 9:6)—indeed, the greatest Prophet of all anticipated by Moses (Deut. 18:15). In the Beatitudes, Jesus shows us the true map to happiness. The destination is unlike all the other roadmaps, however, for they end in God instead of self. In God's roadmap, the way up is the way down; the way to exaltation is through humiliation; the path to true wealth is through spiritual poverty; the way to inherit the earth is through meekness; and the way to be satisfied is to hunger and thirst after righteousness.

Sadly, many people in the professing church today are following the world's roadmaps. There is little distinction between them and the world in their thought life, work life, family life, social life, political life, or even church life. Apathy, worldliness, narcissism, and isolation are rife, as well as theological and moral liberalism. In our day of great apostasy, the Lord alone knows who His people are (2 Tim. 2:19), for the day will reveal who are the identity of the wheat and the tares (Matt. 13:24–30; 1 Cor. 3:13).

The Gospels are at the heart of the Bible, the Sermon on the Mount is at the heart of Matthew, the first Gospel, and the Beatitudes are at the heart of the Sermon on the Mount—so the Beatitudes are at the heart of

Scripture itself. However, while the Beatitudes form arguably one of the most important sections of Scripture, they are also one of the most misunderstood. You see, the Beatitudes do not represent a sociopolitical or economic program, nor a law-code for establishing a works-based righteousness. My good friend and brother, Paulo Junior, shows us in this sobering book that such models of the Beatitudes completely miss (and twist!) the point of this blessed sermon.

Contrary to popular perception, the Beatitudes are neither about Marxist social revolution nor Victorian moralism. They are about Spirit-transformation of the inner man; Jesus was preaching the gospel. Before Jesus expounds the full application of the law in the Sermon on the Mount, he shows us that we are insufficient and only those who have been regenerated and believed the gospel can live a life of gratitude to God. No one can obey the commands of the Sermon on the Mount without a heart change and Spirit-worked transformation. In the Beatitudes, Jesus describes the Christian (and in most of the Beatitudes He essentially describes Himself). One cannot work up these traits in himself because they are so contrary to the natural man. The Beatitudes, then, are gospel-centered and expose our need for Christ.

The Beatitudes are a divinely inspired description of one who has been transformed by the regenerating power of the Holy Spirit and is a citizen of heaven, even while he walks on earth. What does a citizen of heaven look like? He is not of this world; in fact, he thinks and acts totally unlike the world. Instead of being *conformed* to the image of the world, he is *transformed* by the renewing of his mind (Rom. 12:2) and is conformed to the image of Christ (Rom. 8:29). Though not intentionally strange for the wake of countercultural expression, the citizen of heaven is vastly different than unbelievers in a God-glorifying way. He does not follow the trends; he sets a trend which few follow. Jesus compares this citizen of heaven to *salt*, which seasons, cleanses, and preserves, and to *light*—which illuminates and elucidates (Matt. 5:13).

Paulo begins his excellent treatment of the Beatitudes by providing a comprehensive description of Sermon on the Mount: biblical-theological, canonical, historical, religious, and even geographical context. He then shows how Jesus offended some of the most influential segments of first-century Jewish society in His sermon: the Beatitudes would have shocked, angered, and appalled the Pharisees (legalistic formalists and hypocrites), Sadducees (hedonists, skeptics, and rationalists), Essenes (ascetics), and Zealots (nationalists). What each group held in common was their counterfeit and external religion.

Each of the factions that Paulo describes flourish today—in the churches and general societies of Brazil, the United States, and around the globe. The Beatitudes scandalize the Pharisee, the Sadducee, the Essene, and the Zealot in each of us, in our churches, and in our societies. Pay special attention to the author's description of the Sadducee: he is alive and well in our Western culture and has become the dominant religious, political, and social actor since the so-called "Enlightenment." If we are to beware of apostasy, we must beware of the Sadducees' leaven that so quickly infiltrates the church and has cast down many wounded and slain many strong men.

The Beatitudes should shock us in our society, as well—perhaps more so!—and Paulo captures that shock value. The Beatitudes should unsettle us. They break down and turn upside-down every expectation we have for society and the church in our corrupt, depraved, and perverse and twisted generation. The Beatitudes show us that most of what we view as success is failure; and much of what we view as failure is success in God's eyes. Many of the rich in this world are poorer than one can imagine. Many who appear righteous are unrighteous; and it is often the vilest of the vile who are justified in God's eyes for they seek a righteousness outside themselves (Luke 18:14).

Yet it is the full application of the law to the unregenerate heart that makes the gospel so sweet to the awakened sinner. That is the point of the Beatitudes and of the Sermon on the Mount at large. May the Lord use this to raise a new generation of pastors to thunder the law and then bring the sweet honey of the gospel. The blind must first know that they are blind before they seek the One who can give them sight (John 9:41).

Dear friend, as you read Paulo's description of the Beatitudes, let it serve as a litmus test. Ask whether your life resembles the truly transformed person. Do not assume that you are saved simply because you are a member of a church, partake of the sacraments, live a morally upright life, enjoy studying the Bible, or even attend seminary and serve in ministry! One of the most frightening passages of Scripture—also in the Sermon on the Mount—is when the Lord Jesus taught that many on the day of judgment will claim Christ as Lord but have been on the broad way leading to destruction; only those transformed by the Spirit and walking on the narrow way leading to life will be saved (Matt. 7:13–14; 22–24).

As Jesus put it to Nicodemus, "ye must be born again!" (John 3:7). Examine your heart and ask yourself: Am I in the faith? Do I exhibit the kind of radical discipleship of which Jesus spoke? Is my life different than the world, or do I try to live and look like the world in every way short of sinning? If you are saved, the Beatitudes show how we can live a life of *gratitude* in response to God's gracious *deliverance* from our *misery*.

Brother Paulo's exposition of the Beatitudes is scriptural, direct, forceful, and experiential. He writes as he preaches—with fervor, tenderness, compassion, authority, and urgency. His illustrations are practical and well-selected—largely from church history and from life in Brazil, which ought to be interesting for American readers! It is also thoroughly Reformed, magnifying the glory, sovereignty, grace, and mercy of God. Above all, it has significant *evangelistic* value. Perhaps so few come to church and are being saved in our day because Christians do not live the radical, Christlike, cruciform lives that enlighten, preserve, and flavor the world.

Perhaps many who think they are Christians do not proclaim the gospel in evangelism because the gospel has not transformed themselves. They feel like hypocrites to witness to others, for there is little that separates their lives from others. The salt has lost its flavor in such instances (Matt. 5:13). In many ways, there is no wonder that God has not worked in recent years; we have not wanted Him to work, but have been comfortable with our lazy, apathetic, and worldly lives. May God have mercy upon us and cause His face to shine upon us (Psalm 67). May the Holy Spirit work revival in our churches and societies once again—an awakening that surpasses the First and Second Great Awakenings in the United States!

Now listen to the preface of the greatest sermon of all time from the greatest Preacher of all time—the Lord Jesus Christ—with reverence, expectation, anticipation, and dependence on the Holy Spirit. Tremble as you open the pages of Scripture and ponder the meditations that Paulo has penned for your consideration. You must either be salted here by life-transformation or you will be seasoned with fire in the pains of everlasting destruction if you do not repent and believe the gospel (Mark 9:49). Christ calls us to radical discipleship—truly life-transforming, inside-out heart change that impacts our relationships, families, children, work, relationship to neighbors, the government, and even our enemies.

One can only be a true disciple of Jesus if the Holy Spirit has regenerated him through faith in the gospel. Where are the men of God? Where are ministers who live as they speak? Where are men and women who look and live like Jesus Christ? Where are those who hunger and thirst after righteousness? May the Lord be pleased to pour out His Spirit afresh and work in our hearts for His name's sake.

—**Joel R. Beeke**
Chancellor and Professor of Systematic Theology and Homiletics, *Puritan Reformed Theological Seminary*
Pastor, *Heritage Reformed Congregation of Grand Rapids, Michigan*—Grand Rapids, Michigan

Introduction

My desire to write this book came from preaching a series of expositions on the Beatitudes in my local church. During a long period of detailed study of Matthew 5, especially the first thirteen verses, I became sad and perplexed when I realized that many Christians today no longer possess the biblical characteristics of a genuine follower of Jesus found in this passage and have distanced themselves considerably from what he intended for them.

Today there is a vast number of groups and various denominations with thousands of members calling themselves Christians, however they lead their lives in a way that is incompatible with the faith they claim to profess. This could either be due to the lack of true conversion or because of pure ignorance of the high standard that the Word of God commands from his people. The urgent redemption of the Christian identity is therefore necessary.

Christians must be pure, holy, and distinct from the world, for a holy people point to a holy God. It is with these true markers of Christian identification that we witness the beauty and majesty of God to the world. The opposite of this dishonors him, offends him, and diminishes his glory. We are seeing the Christian walk, in broad steps, moving towards "secularization," which makes it quite difficult to distinguish between the Christian and the non-Christian.

In this book I will provide a clear analysis of the character of the true Christian: how they should live, the fundamental characteristics that mark a Christian, and how the manifestation of these characteristics in the life of a Christian will impact the society in which they live. The Beatitudes speak exactly to these points.

The Beatitudes are found within the Sermon on the Mount which was delivered by the Lord of glory, Jesus Christ. In a certain part of that sermon, Jesus illustrates his teaching with salt: if it has lost its savor, it is good for nothing (Matt 5:13). Christ was saying that salt, in order to truly be salt, should possess all the properties that constitute it as salt, in order to give flavor and preserve the foods from corruption. If it simply looked like salt but didn't possess those specific properties, it is not true salt.

Jesus said, in short, that we—Christians—are "the salt of the earth" and, as salt, it is our duty to influence the world (give taste), to form opinions, to set trends, and live a lifestyle to be copied. However, how can this be done? In my view, for salt to truly be salt, it must have the properties of salt; so for Christians, to truly be Christians, they must have the characteristics of the Christian. What distinctive marks are these? What is the character of the true Christian? The Beatitudes portray those marks, which, if manifested in our daily lives, make us capable of changing society around us.

The life of a true Christian has the capability to powerfully influence fallen humanity and curb corruption, simply by portraying Christlikeness to the world. Think for a moment of the Puritans of the 17th century. Consider how they worshiped, how they lived, how authentic they were! Study them and understand how they expressed the Beatitudes in their lives. And more: note how much the Puritans influenced the society that surrounded them. Dear reader, this is exactly what the Savior, Jesus Christ, exhorts you to do.

My prayer is that this book contributes to the edification of the church of Christ and of every sincere Christian—helping to recovering their unique character and their true biblical identity, praising God and exalting his glory.

Soli Deo Gloria!

Paulo Junior
May 2017

CHAPTER 1

The Sermon on the Mount

The Sermon on the Mount is arguably the greatest doctrinal and practical discourse of the Lord Jesus Christ. It is composed of solid and detailed doctrine with consistent practical application. It is, of course, the greatest sermon ever written proclaimed by the greatest preacher to ever exist: Jesus Christ.

This unique text occupies a place of prominence and honor in the heart of every Christian tradition over the last two thousand years—in prayers, in preaching, and in studies. If we refer to politics, we will see that many presidential or parliamentary speeches have used quotations from the Sermon on the Mount, an example of how its lessons are fascinating and admirable to the secular world. There is no doubt of the great significance of the Sermon on the Mount.

However, no other part of Sacred Scripture has suffered as much misinterpretation, as much exegetical and hermeneutical distortion, as the Sermon on the Mount.

By way of example: the misinterpretation of "blessed are the poor" (Matt 5:3) by Francis of Assisi (1182–1226) led to the Roman Catholic teaching that physical poverty— deprivation of material possessions—was synonymous with piety; this caused the creation of orders of miserable people who had taken vows of poverty in search of a sanctified life. It was believed that the abstention of comfort, luxury, and material possessions granted entry into the kingdom of Heaven.

If there are already dangers in the interpretation of the Sermon on the Mount, how can we avoid making new mistakes such as the one above? How can we know what this great sermon consists of, with its Christocentric and evangelical doctrine? How can we avoid an incorrect or even false interpretation of the Sermon on the Mount? How is it possible to know the truth of what Jesus is teaches? It is only through the study of Scripture as a whole; we can never analyze a text in isolation without taking into account the other parts of the Bible. The interpretation of the text, in particular the Sermon on the Mount, needs to begin in the general and move to the particular, that is, from the whole doctrine of the Bible to this specific passage.

Dr. Martyn Lloyd-Jones (1899–1981) taught that one should analyze the Sermon on the Mount remembering that it was not the only thing Christ taught. Therefore, for a correct interpretation of the sermon, we need to know and compare the other teachings of Jesus, both before and after the Sermon on the Mount. We also need to regard the rest of the content of the New Testament, passing through the Gospels, Acts of the Apostles, the writings of Paul, James, Peter, John, Jude, and, even, the book of Revelation. And more: we need to have before us the teaching of the Old Testament, so that we can understand how many conclusions which appear in the New Testament were formed under the old covenant. Therefore, our method in the exposition of the character of the true Christian will be to study the Beatitudes and to compare them with other texts from the whole Bible in order to come to a unified understanding of God's revelation of the distinct character of the Christian.

Before going into the Beatitudes themselves to discover the character of the true Christian, it is very important for us to lay the introductory groundwork of the Sermon on the Mount as a whole, marking important points for its interpretation and the correct application for the Christian life today.

The message from the Sermon on the Mount

When analyzing the text of the Sermon on the Mount, even an inattentive reader will soon realize that the principles of truth mine far deeper than simply ethics and morals. The sermon speaks of forgiveness and love in a way that is almost intolerable; it teaches about righteousness at an extraordinary level, even for the most charitable social standards that have ever existed; it confronts purity in relationships, penetrating man's most hidden thoughts and ideas. The sonorous harmonies of the symphony that is the Sermon on the Mount soars high above the simple melody of human morality and ethics. This is how it should be.

The sermon contains the doctrinal and practical teaching of the new society, of the new witnesses, and of the new covenant of God in Christ Jesus. The people who would receive the message and be its message-bearers—a calling which would reshape their entire existence thereafter—should shine with an unmistakable light amidst deep darkness, both in that day and today.

What is the unique message of the Sermon on the Mount? That the righteous life before God begins from the inside out. It is the message of radical change on the inside, requiring renewal and transformation—a true and complete revolution. The Sermon on the Mount declares war on the fallen and corrupt heart of every son and daughter of Adam—of every impenitent sinner. It pervades the mind, the will, and the innermost thoughts of every human being, laying them bare before God's holy divinity. With his sermon, Christ calls all men everywhere to repent and conform to the standard of God's kingdom.

Have you ever imagined how this message fell on the hearts of Jesus's listeners at that time? It was as if he had said: "I have not come to bring more religious rules, neither a social revolution, nor insurrection against Rome, or increase in wages, or land and worldly possessions. Forget hate, bloody wars, silent conspiracies and the restoration of a physical kingdom; my foundations are love, forgiveness, reconciliation, mercy, justice, purity, bravery, and tenderness."

Perhaps the astonished crowd mumbled, "What? What did you say? Is it all to do with repentance, love, poverty, and simplicity? Please repeat! Will the kingdom be enjoyed in eternity and not today? Is there a heavy cross to be carried and a narrow path to follow our whole lives?"

Would that not be the reason why the Sermon on the Mount was so admired from the time it was delivered, but so little practiced, to the present day? His message continues to be an acid for the flesh; however, for those made as subjects of the kingdom of God, it is beautiful, just, and totally desirable, for it is a portrait of the King of this kingdom.

The Constitution of a Distinct People

When God called Abram from Ur of the Chaldeans, he instituted with him a pact—a covenant—to make him into a great nation, through which all the families of the earth would be blessed (Gen 12:1–3). Through the revelation of God and of his covenant with Abraham, there was the constitution of a people distinguished from others, chosen and separated by God for a specific purpose: to be his representative on earth.

They would be considered God's people, the race of God, exclusive property of God. For such, their customs would be different from other peoples; their laws, their garments, their relationships, their way of worshiping God, and their purpose would be distinct, aimed at honoring and pleasing the One who had called them.

God's covenant was extended to the descendants of Abraham, Isaac, and Jacob, and then to the twelve sons of Jacob, who became the twelve tribes of Israel. With the arrival of Moses, the Law was given as a code of precepts and rules that satisfied the terms of the covenant between God and his own people (Exod 6:7; Lev 22:33; Num 15:41).

While the Law of Moses was the code of faith and practice for the people of God of the Old Testament, the Sermon on the Mount was the doctrinal and behavioral constitution for the church of the New Testament. On its foundation, the personal, public, and community life of the church of God would be erected, appearing as a testimony of a distinct people: the light of the world (Matt 5:14–16).

Just as in the Old Testament where the Jewish people had been God's witness to the lost world (Isa 43:12, 44:8), the new people of the kingdom of God (Gal 3:9)—made up of the saved of all peoples, languages, and nations—are God's witnesses to the world. The church is the Lord's own property, which points to the righteousness, holiness, perfection, and majesty of God (1 Pet 2:9). Therefore, the Sermon on the Mount is the law of this new people of God, who believe and live in a way that obeys the Law of Christ, imitating his character and behaving according to his conduct as a perfect man.

The theological context of the Sermon on the Mount

The Sermon on the Mount is found in its entirety in the gospel according to Matthew, even though there are passages of it in the gospel of Luke (ch. 6). The gospel of Matthew is the first book of the New Testament and is the first of the four Gospels, so it was not placed in this order by chance.

Let us look at the theological context of the time. Israel had not received any divine messages though a prophet for four hundred years. It had been four hundred years since God had spoken to his people by written or spoken word; four hundred years without sending the messenger (promised in Mal 4:5–6); four hundred years maintaining a deep silence of revelation.

The whole nation of Israel was under the ancient covenant. They were awaiting the fulfillment of the prophecies of the old covenant, and, above all, those concerning the coming, birth, and manifestation of their Messiah.

With all of this anticipation, what was the purpose of the first gospel? Why was this book written and why was the Sermon on the Mount included in it? Matthew wanted to prove that God's silence had been broken. He wanted to prove that God would again talk to his people. With that first gospel, Matthew proves that God broke the silence of revelation precisely with the coming of the Messiah, and that the Messiah was Jesus Christ.

Matthew is the most Jewish book of the four gospels. It is a gospel written especially to the people of Israel, referencing their habits, history, and religion. The gospel of Matthew was written in a style that the Jewish audience would clearly recognize, with illustrations and arguments that were easy to understand and apply. His great message, therefore, was to announce that the silence had been broken, the messenger who would prepare the way for the Messiah was sent, the Messiah was already on earth, and this Messiah was Jesus of Nazareth.

The gospel of Matthew, therefore, is the bond between the Old Testament and the New Testament. For this reason, in this gospel we find more quotations from the Old Testament than in any other. His message is an announcement to the Jewish remnant—those who were awaiting the fulfillment of the prophecies—that Jesus Christ was both God and man, fulfilling the word given in the Old Testament.

This is the gospel in which we find the Sermon on the Mount, and it is in the Sermon on the Mount that the depiction of the earthly life and ministry of the newly arrived Messiah is contained. Jesus first came to the people of Israel, but they did not have a very clear idea of the nature of the messianic kingdom. Precisely for this reason, Jesus made so many connections to the Old Testament in the Sermon on the Mount, so that the Jewish people could recognize the character of the kingdom of God and Jesus as his sent Messiah.

The setting for the Sermon on the Mount

The Sermon on the Mount was delivered in a specific period of history, probably between the year 30 and 31 AD. At that time, there were many things happening in the lives of the inhabitants of Judea under Roman rule. To better understand Jesus's discourse in this sermon, we need to understand some details of the people of that time, their religion and expectations.

The expectation of the Jewish people of that time

What did most of the Israelites expect from the Messiah? They were waiting for a military and political leader. In fact, the people's great expectation was that the Messiah would instigate political reform by organizing a military endeavor against Caesar, to take away the yoke Rome had over Israel.

The dream of that people was that under the Messiah's government, Israel would have greater glories and victories than it had in the kingdoms of David and Solomon. They believed that the Messiah would come to bring political, social, and economic reform, which would bring Israel out of foreign domination and restore its glory and power.

In this very context Jesus appeared and began to perform signs and wonders throughout Galilee that nobody else had done. He soon began to be hailed as the Messiah of the prophecies. However, when Jesus went up the mountain and began preaching the Sermon on the Mount, there must have been a mixture of admiration and frustration among the people.

Those gathered were likely full of admiration because of the profound nature of the sermon, full of power and such grace that in the end the people who heard it "were amazed at his doctrine: for he taught them as one having authority and not as their scribes" (Matt 7:28–29). However, there was likely frustration too, that the sermon held a frank rebuke to any war of liberation against the Romans; it was contrary to revenge, social reform, and quick resolution. The sermon spoke of reform in the heart, the need for the desires and inclinations of the hearts of mankind to be changed.

The ideals preached in the Sermon on the Mount were totally contrary to those which the Jews expected. They were waiting for a speech like those made in Berlin—the temple of Nazism—by Adolf Hitler (1889–1945). They were expecting a triumphant and positive speech, of life or death for their homeland.

But that was not Jesus's speech in this sermon. Jesus spoke meekly, touching on sensitive points of inner change; he spoke of reconciliation, submission, and subjection. In that sermon, Christ's proposal was not to change in any way the physical, political, or economic aspects of the nation. They were the words of abandoning revolts, leaving swords, exalting what the entire world despised, and to despise all that the world exalted. These were words that were diametrically opposed to what the Israelites of the time expected.

It was a paradoxical sermon, which the fallen human mind could not receive. The Beatitudes were a shock and scandal for the natural mind. For example, "Blessed are they that mourn" (Matt 5:4). How would a carnal mind understand that? Someone would say, "What? Blessed, happy, and correct is the one who mourns? The world teaches that happy are those who laughs!" Society exalted the lifestyles of the rich and famous aristocracy. Jesus exalted the publicans, the harlots, and the sinners, rejecting what society and culture loved.

Imagine the thoughts of the Pharisees and Sadducees: "What are you saying?! God has not spoken for four hundred years and, now, he has sent this guy to declare that he is the Messiah? Son of a carpenter, from Nazareth in Galilee, of those despised and insignificant people? We expected an authentic military successor of David, who would come in an imposing cavalry with his well-trained army, prepared to lead us to the glory we once had!"

No, that was not Jesus's proposal for the kingdom of God! He stated categorically when asked by the Roman governor, Pontius Pilate, "My kingdom is not of this world: If my kingdom were of this world, then would my servants fight, that I should not be delivered to the Jews: but now my kingdom is not from hence" (John 18:36).

The Sermon on the Mount, therefore, stated that the kingdom of Jesus would not yet be of this world. Thrones and riches would not yet be here, but rather the desires of the subjects of this kingdom would change—their expectations would change.

Dear reader, think about it: what do you expect from the kingdom of God? Do you expect your personal ambitions to be fulfilled and the life of health and prosperity advertised by the present culture to be your reward in following Jesus? Beware, you will be as frustrated with the kingdom of God as were the first-century Jews.

The religion of the Jewish people of that time

Just as the expectations of the Jewish people of Jesus's time were diverse, in the same way their beliefs and values were very complex. The religious leaders of that period in Israel were divided basically into four groups: the Pharisees, Sadducees, Essenes, and Zealots.

The Pharisees

The Pharisees made up the traditional wing, which had a great deal of prestige among the population due to their aim of redeeming and reviving the religious ideals of the Jewish nation. This group held that Judaism must consist in keeping the commandments of the Old Testament as well as the customs that many rabbis added to the Law of Moses.

They made several additions to the Law of the Old Testament, bolstered by the argument that they wanted to serve God in a purer way. They were legalistic men who were more zealous for the tradition than for the true worship of God. The Pharisees taught the fact, albeit untrue, that salvation was obtained by external good deeds and mercy proven by strict obedience to the Law.

On account of this, Jesus said that this group diminished God's Word through their own tradition (Mark 7:13). The Pharisees worshiped and obeyed the tradition of the rabbinical leaders more than God's own Law!

Jesus knew the hearts of these leaders, and his response in the Sermon on the Mount taught the Pharisees that true spirituality, true religion, was not based on external deeds. The Apostle Paul himself said they were dedicated to the law and purity of doctrine, but not in the correct way, "for I bear them record that they have a zeal of God, but not according to knowledge" (Rom 10:2).

Jesus also taught that the devotions of the Pharisees consisted only of deeds that were public. They sought a hypocritical religion that was fueled by the recognition of society, but not the pure religion that flowed from a heart grateful to God for his forgiveness (Luke 18:10–14).

Below are some reprimands of Jesus in the Sermon on the Mount against the external religion of the Pharisees:

> Therefore when thou doest thine alms, do not sound a trumpet before thee, as the hypocrites do in the synagogues and in the streets, that they may have glory of men. Verily I say unto you, They have their reward. (Matt 6:2)

> And when thou prayest, thou shalt not be as the hypocrites are: for they love to pray standing in the synagogues and in the corners of the streets, that they may be seen of men. (Matt 6:5)

> But when ye pray, use not vain repetitions, as the heathen do: for they think that they shall be heard for their much speaking. (Matt 6:7)

> Moreover when ye fast, be not, as the hypocrites, of a sad countenance: for they disfigure their faces, that they may appear unto men to fast. (Matt 6:16)

While the Pharisees bragged about a religion that sought to demonstrate piety for men, the Sermon on the Mount emphasized that public offerings (alms) do not please God, but rather secretive donations (Matt 6:3–4); that the pompous prayers in public were not the standard accepted by God, but private prayer (Matt 6:6); that the extensive and repeated prayers were no more pleasing to God than the simple and sincere personal prayers (Matt 6:9–15); and that the fasting prayers received by God should be offered in secret (Matt 6:17–18).

All the formidable acts of worship that the Pharisees presented had a common problem: they was not sincere, and they did not come from a transformed life that led to righteous practice. It was their vain intention to be accepted for the many things they were doing and not for the devotion of the heart.

The Sadducees

The Sadducees were almost the opposite of the Pharisees. They could be correctly identified as the "liberal wing" of Judaism. They were immediatists, libertine, and were not so concerned with spiritual piety. They believed in only a small portion of the Old Testament, restricted to the most convenient aspects of the Law of Moses. They ignored the tradition of the rabbis and much of God's teaching through the prophets and historical books. For example, they did not believe in angels, in the soul or in life after death, in miracles, or in the final resurrection.

Their religion was based on "living in the here and now," precisely the same teaching that Paul rebuked, years later in Corinth: "If the dead rise not? let us eat and drink; for to morrow we die" (1Cor 15:32b).

Jesus also knew the hearts of these leaders, and in the Sermon on the Mount he taught the Sadducees that their rationale and licentiousness were contrary to the spirit of faith and piety.

Here is an interesting contrast: the legalistic Pharisees thought they would be approved by the volume of obedience to the Law; the Sadducees did not. They were not concerned with obedience; they were the libertines—immoral and carnal—living by the rationale: "since life does not promise anything after death, we can do whatever we want."

Jesus had a hard rebuke in the Sermon on the Mount for the liberal Sadducees as well: "Ye are the salt of the earth: but if the salt have lost his savour, wherewith shall it be salted? It is thenceforth good for nothing, but to be cast out, and to be trodden under foot of men" (Matt 5:13).

Jesus taught that if the salt does not contain the properties which make it salt, it is not salt. It was like saying that the Sadducees had no characteristics of true religion (the salt) in their lives. A disciple of Jesus Christ could not deny the resurrection, the necessity of godly living, and sanctification. A true follower of Christ could not live a life without piety and dedication to God.

Jesus concluded, therefore, that if the Sadducees did not possess the essential characteristics of the true religion they would have no quality that would preserve them from suffering God's judgment and would be thrown out of his presence. In their condition, they would not be saved on the day of the final judgment.

The Essenes

Another group of Jews on the scene during the time of Christ's ministry was the Essenes. The Essenes were a Jewish religious group living in isolated communities. They were ascetics who made many vows of self-discipline, seeking to despise the body and passions of human nature, similar to the monks of the Middle Ages. They understood that pure religion, that piety, was the total separation from society to a life of strict isolation.

They lived far from Jerusalem and from the populous centers, in distant places, thinking that their isolation would give them spiritual gain. Their firm foundation was that being apart from the world would guarantee them some kind of superior sanctification.

Jesus had words of address for them in the Sermon on the Mount as well. Jesus taught the Essenes that piety should come from the inside and not from the outside. While the Essenes believed that self-flagellation and self-punishment were the cause of gain, acceptance, and sanctification, Jesus said, "Blessed are the pure in heart" (Matt 5:8).

It is as if Jesus said, "All of this you are doing is deeply impressive, however your heart does not change; you are still bad, stingy, judgmental and vain."

The teaching of the Sermon on the Mount made it clear that sanctification should begin with a right heart towards God, so that the external actions would be purified. Sanctification does not occur for those who are not in Christ, but rather for those who have been accepted by Christ.

The Zealots

The final Jewish group we will address in this section is the Zealots, the radical activists or the nationalist fanatics of that time. For them there was no other way to serve the Lord but to take up weapons and stand up against the Roman Empire. As a group that incited revolts, they believed that they would establish the kingdom by the sword; in their minds, the kingdom of the Messiah would only be established by means of war and bloodshed.

In the Sermon on the Mount, Jesus taught the Zealots that the greatest revolution to be accomplished would not be with weapons and much outpouring of blood, but through a humble, holy, and peaceful posture.

The Zealots were eager for the arrival of the Messiah, so that the trumpet might finally be played and the order for a great fight against all the powers that oppressed the Jewish people would be given. Instead Jesus came and taught, "love your enemies, bless them that curse you, do good to them that hate you, and pray for them which despitefully use you, and persecute you" (Matt 5:44).

The Zealots must have been completely disappointed with Jesus: "What? Are you telling me that I have to love Caesar, Pilate, and Herod? And that I have to pray for them?" In fact, the doctrine of Jesus was radically opposed to the inclinations of this Jewish group.

After a brief overview of these groups, the complex background of the Jewish religion of that period could be summarized as: the Pharisees as fierce traditionalists; the Sadducees as liberals; the Essenes as separatists; and the Zealots as revolutionary activists. However, using the Jewish faith to promote their own interests was what they all held in common.

In which of these groups do you think Jesus's posture, ethics, and religion would fit? In none of them. All of these groups were mistaken in their positions as to the true religion. They were in complete disagreement with the new covenant of grace being established.

The preacher of the Sermon on the Mount

We do not need vast biblical knowledge to know who the tremendous preacher of this sermon was: Jesus Christ.

It is possible that you have already heard, watched, or read several sermons that have marked your life and have been stamped on your memory. Perhaps you have heard of many powerful preachers of the gospel, such as Charles Haddon Spurgeon (1834–1892), known as the "Prince of Preachers," or even Jonathan Edwards (1703–1758), the preacher of the well-known sermon "Sinners in the Hands of an Angry God," which was preached more than two hundred and seventy years ago and is still discussed today.

However, there is something different and special about the Sermon on the Mount and its preacher. The one who preached it is the greatest preacher of all time who preached the greatest sermon of all time! This preacher was Emmanuel, which means "God is with us, the present God." It was God, in flesh, who delivered his message to mankind.

Why is it significant that the preacher of the Sermon on the Mount was God? Because Jesus Christ is God, there was no confusion in his speech, no exaggeration, no misconceptions—all of which occur with human preachers, even with the greatest of them. When Jesus preached the Sermon on the Mount, his Word was inspired, infallible, and inerrant. What he spoke was the divine, canonical Word to all humanity.

The preacher of this sermon is the God who truly knew man. It was he who created man, and he knew exactly what he was saying in the sermon about them. Jesus has been with mankind since the creation, following their falls, virtues, and development. This preacher cross-examined the heart of man, and he did not need to assume anything, because—as the omnicscient God—he wholly knew the hearts of each person.

D. Martyn Lloyd-Jones once said that preaching is "the truth transmitted through the personality." Thus, it is possible to know a lot about the preacher's life through his sermons. His inclinations, conduct, and his values are exposed through the mode, content, and delivery of his sermons.

In the case of the Sermon on the Mount, we see that this sermon clearly reflects the personality of Jesus. It is characterized by Christ's holiness, righteousness, purity, and integrity. In this sermon you find the values of God and his conduct while incarnate on Earth. You are exposed to the heart of Christ in this sermon, revealing his will and character.

The conclusion of the sermon records the following: "And it came to pass, when Jesus had ended these sayings, the people were astonished at his doctrine: For he taught them as one having authority, and not as the scribes" (Matt 7:28–29). This passage is conclusive in showing the character of the preacher. Why were the crowds amazed at Jesus's preaching? Because he did not teach or preach as the scribes, but as someone who had authority. The crowds, in making this comment, were comparing the character of the preachers: on one side Jesus the God-man, and on the other, the scribes whose teachings were filled with hypocrisy.

People could see that the scribes had no authority, strength, or backing; they did not portray life, because their messages expressed a superficial, petty, dry, and cold character. But when they heard Jesus's preaching, the crowds noticed that he preached as someone who had virtue, power, warmth, grace, light, and love.

In addition, the way Jesus preached the Sermon on the Mount had a profound impact on the crowd: "And seeing the multitudes, he went up into a mountain: and when he was set, his disciples came unto him" (Matt 5:1). Jesus taught sitting down. Matthew made a point of recording in his account that before Jesus delivered the Sermon on the Mount he sat down. Why did Jesus do this? Why would he speak while seated?

It was common practice in the time of Jesus that rabbis, the teachers of religion, taught sitting down. When someone taught standing up—in the squares or in the houses—it meant that that teaching was informal; it was a common teaching, not to be received as a decree. However, when they sat down, the teaching became formal.

A passage that exemplifies this is found in Matthew 23:2: "the Scribes and the Pharisees sit in Moses' seat." If the Pharisees were teaching standing up, it would be somewhat informal, however, if they were seated, the teaching would have greater importance. Therefore, teaching seated in Moses's seat was equivalent to saying that the Pharisees were teaching under the authority of Moses and that what they said was an official message of the Law. That was the ex cathedra teaching—teaching on the basis of the seat (the title or the position) and of the authority.

For example, when the Pope teaches something ex cathedra, it means that the teaching is considered an infallible, authorized word that must be included in the Canonical Roman Catholic Code, leading all Catholic followers to follow as a divine order—even though truly it is not!

Thus, when Jesus went up the mountain, sat down and proclaimed the sermon, it was explicit to all those present that it was the infallible, official, and authoritative Word of the kingdom of God. It was teaching that had the importance and seal of the Messiah. Jesus knew exactly what he was doing and the effect it had on his audience. Remember that the sermon was being delivered to Jewish listeners, accustomed to immediately identify that a master seated was teaching with authority and as a decree of God.

In short, Jesus preached with the authority of the Messiah, of the author of the kingdom of God. His words were divine, which should be received as decrees of the most High by all who hear them.

The place where the Sermon on the Mount was preached

It was not a mere coincidence that the sermon was proclaimed on a mount, although the Bible does not mention the specific mount or geographic location. Why was the great sermon for the inauguration of the kingdom of God and the institution of his law spoken on a mount? Why did Jesus choose a mount on which to preach this specific sermon?

Jesus did this to create a parallel, a connection with Moses and the institution of the Old Testament law. All of the Holy Law, brought to Israel, came from God's revelation to Moses on a mount (see Exod 19 et seq.). So that the Jews might heed closely what Jesus was saying, the sermon was strategically pronounced on a mount, as it was with Moses.

However, Jesus's discourse was not the same as Moses's discourse. When he went up the mount to speak, Jesus was not repeating the Law of Moses, with all of the sacrifices and rituals of worship. His teaching pointed to the complete fulfillment of that law in him. Jesus stated that the shadows that the Law represented had now passed, and its total fulfillment had come (see Col 2:16–23 and Heb 10).

With those words, a new law—a new covenant—was being proclaimed to the people. The promulgation of a new divine decree was taking place, so Jesus gave it as he was seated on a mount, showing his authority as the legislator and Messiah of Israel.

In addition, the use of a mount for the sermon would resemble the place where the new covenant would be ratified: the mount of crucifixion. With his crucifixion on a mount, the terms of God's new covenant with man were sealed. It was there that Jesus received upon his life the curse and condemnation of the Law of God for the sins of men (Isa 53). When Jesus climbed the mount called Calvary, the tablets of God's righteous Law, with their judgments and convictions, fell on him so that through his work God's justification could rest on those who repent and believe in Him (Rom 3:23–26).

In this way, the act of Jesus going up the mount served both to fulfill the Law of God, bearing the full accursed load, and imputing the righteousness of God upon believers through his amazing grace.

The listeners of the Sermon on the Mount

To whom were the words of the Sermon on the Mount addressed? Those listening comprised two distinct groups: the disciples and the crowd.

The Sermon on the Mount was directed to the disciples (Matt 5:1) as a teaching of the character of the true Christian, so that they would understand and recognize the conduct, motivations, and principles that would rule the lives of those who were saved by God.

If you remember, Jesus's first message to those who came to believe in him was not a set of commandments that, if they followed them, they would be saved. Not at all! The first message of Jesus to those who would become his disciples was a call to repentance and faith, as recorded in Mark 1:15: "the time is fulfilled, and the kingdom of God is at hand: repent ye, and believe the gospel."

The Sermon on the Mount was delivered to those who would repent and believe, for those who were called by God. They were the saved—those who were made disciples of Christ and who had entered into the kingdom of God. With the Sermon on the Mount they were receiving the constitution, the commandments of the kingdom of heaven, that they might observe them.

In addition to Christ's disciples, a vast crowd was present (Matt 5:1). Among them were men and women in need of salvation who had not yet heard the message of the Lord Jesus. In this regard, for the multitude, the Sermon on the Mount was evangelistic. See what Matthew 7:13–14 says, "Enter ye in at the strait gate: for wide is the gate, and broad is the way, that leadeth to destruction, and many there be which go in thereat: Because strait is the gate, and narrow is the way, which leadeth unto life, and few there be that find it."

To follow the narrow path of the gospel was to follow Christ. It was an urgent call of the Lord to abandon religious error and to move towards obedience in faith. He was teaching that the kingdom of God was not for everyone, but for those to leave the wide gate and broad path and to go through the narrow door, walking down its tight path. In that sermon, therefore, the crowd is also called to repentance, to believe in the gospel of salvation.

Before concluding this topic, you must be aware of two things:

First, although the Sermon on the Mount contains an invitation to repentance and faith, the practice of its teachings does not generate, by the act of fulfilling them, anyone's salvation.

Some, throughout the history of the Church, have taught that the sermon showed the way of salvation through obedience. They said, "Do you want to be saved? Fulfill the Sermon on the Mount!" They taught that salvation would come by observing the Beatitudes (Matt 5:3–11), that is, people should be merciful and meek peacemakers, following with pure hearts, hungry and thirsty for righteousness—and thereby reach the standard for God's salvation.

However, this aspect is not correct in any way, for if it were so, salvation could be achieved by works, denying Ephesians 2:8–9: "For by grace are ye saved through faith; and that not of yourselves: it is the gift of God; not of works, lest any man should boast."

The truth throughout the Bible is that salvation comes from an act of God, not as a reward to men for their qualities and achievements, but by grace and faith alone. Someone is saved not by merit for practicing the teachings of the Sermon on the Mount. Rather, because someone has really been saved, they can truly be a practitioner of the Sermon on the Mount and have in themselves the marks of a true Christian, which are the Beatitudes.

Secondly, there were others claiming that the Sermon on the Mount could not be fulfilled, even by Christians, while they were still in this world. This line of teaching would state that the Sermon on the Mount would have a secondary and future application, only possible to be fulfilled in the Millennium and in eternity. With this doctrine, it was sustained that no Christian would be able to fulfill the Sermon on the Mount, which makes the sermon a beautiful model of the ideal, but not something to be actively sought by Christians while in this corrupt world.

There is a fundamental error in stating such a thing: salvation, with the justification of the sinner, is an immediate act that completely changes the life of the person and their eternal position when it occurs. For a saved person, eternity has already started and they already enjoy part of God's glory on this side of heaven.

Therefore, even if the saved are not sanctified completely and perfected in this life, a portion of God's purity and righteousness is given to every man and woman when they are saved (1 Cor 1:30–31). This salvation matures, being progressively and continually perfected throughout the life of the Christian (2 Pet 1:10), which allows the Christian to fulfill even more the content of the Sermon on the Mount.

The Sermon on the Mount does not say: "Blessed are the poor in spirit, because theirs will be the kingdom of God" (Matt 5:3). On the contrary, Jesus states that the kingdom of God is already of the humble/poor in spirit; they inherit the kingdom now, not in the future. They are already part of the Lord's holy people; the principle of the kingdom of God is already within in them.

Therefore, for those who have passed from death to life, who are new creatures (2 Cor 5:17), renewed in the image of the One who created them, the kingdom of God with his work of transformation has already begun to operate powerfully in their hearts, empowering them to grow even more in the likeness of the Lord Jesus (Prov 4:18; Rom 8:29).

A test of true salvation

Before ending this brief panorama of the Sermon on the Mount, a word of exhortation needs to be given.

The Sermon on the Mount has great usefulness in attesting and proving whether regeneration has occurred in the life of a person which leads to salvation. By studying this sermon, someone will be confronted with the standard of conduct expected by God from a loyal subject of his heavenly kingdom.

In order for someone to be a Christian, the law of the new covenant must be carved into the tablets of their heart. What is this law? The principles taught by Jesus in the Sermon on the Mount. This preaching of Jesus distinguishes the new Israel, the church, from the other peoples. When Moses came down with the Law from Sinai (Exod 20), it was written on stone tablets; with the Sermon on the Mount, the "Law of Grace" was written on the heart of the faithful. Thus, Christians are walking tablets, walking books wherever they go, having the Law of God manifested in their daily lives.

When studying the Sermon on the Mount, a person can only come to two conclusions: either they are approved or they fail; either someone is indeed living the life of a saved person, with evidence of the principles of the Sermon on the Mount in their thoughts, conversation, conduct, and desires, or they are not. There is no room for doubt.

The question is: are you a new creation? Does your life reflect the teachings of the Sermon on the Mount? Is your heart clean? Are your intents holy? Do you walk along the narrow path? Does the gospel cost you—are you dying daily to the world, to sin, and to Satan's temptations? Do you have great joy for the righteousness of God and in communion with his faithful people, or is the world still the source of your greatest enjoyment? The standards proclaimed in the Sermon on the Mount confirm whether a person in fact passed through the narrow gate (salvation) and walks along the narrow path (sanctification). The Sermon on the Mount shows the urgent need for new birth in the life of an unregenerate person.

When reading these following verses, a person realizes that they have no strength for such a high standard of living. It is impossible for these standards to be fulfilled by their own strength of will:

If any man will sue thee at the law, and take away thy coat, let him have thy cloak also. And whosoever shall compel thee to go a mile, go with him twain. (Matt 5:40–41)

Ye have heard that it hath been said, Thou shalt love thy neighbour, and hate thine enemy. But I say unto you, Love your enemies, bless them that curse you, do good to them that hate you, and pray for them which despitefully use you, and persecute you. (Matt 5:43–44)

Forgive us our debts, just as we have forgiven our debtors. (Matt 6:12)

Lay not up for yourselves treasures upon earth, where moth and rust doth corrupt, and where thieves break through and steal: but lay up for yourselves treasures in heaven, where neither moth nor rust doth corrupt, and where thieves do not break through nor steal. (Matt 6:19–20)

This person is aware that in their own strength, they do not have patience and willingness to do everything for their neighbor; they cannot love those who have done evil to them and forgive those who have been guilty of offending them; they cannot leave earthly ambitions with a view to the eternal rest of the saints in heaven.

In this sermon Jesus is teaching that love must be unconditional—for the wife, children, murderers, cowards, and the people who have hurt them most. Patience and willingness must go far beyond mere convenience. Forgiveness must be independent of the level of the offense. You must forgive those who have verbally attacked you or those who have shot you. The ambitions of this world must be joyfully lost in favor of the hope of the future reward in heaven with Christ. When someone understands this truth, they may be shocked, realizing that this is not the reality of their will and conduct.

As you can see, the Sermon on the Mount shows the depravity, misery, and sinfulness of the human being. It shows how much man has degenerated due to the Fall into sin. The sermon shows that, without a supernatural work of the Holy Spirit of God, no one can be saved (Jonah 2:9).

Another aspect that the Sermon on the Mount highlights is the witness, the conduct of the Christian before society. Perhaps you who are reading may ask yourself, "Why do the people I am witnessing to not becoming Christians? Why do they not show any interest in the Christian faith or in the church?" It is possible that your life—if you are not practicing the teaching of the Sermon on the Mount—contradicts the words that you speak? The misconduct of a Christian speaks much more loudly than their words. Your lifestyle and witness can both confirm and ruin the Christianity you profess. We see an example of this in the New Testament: "And [I Paul] was unknown by face unto the churches of Judaea which were in Christ: But they had heard only, that he which persecuted us in times past now preacheth the faith which once he destroyed. And they glorified God in me" (Gal 1:22–24).

Do you remember who Saul of Tarsus was? The merciless Jewish Pharisee who persecuted and desolated the church of Christ. The wild man who breathed out threats against the disciples (Acts 9:1). That ancient and cruel enemy had become a born-again Christian! And what happened? His conduct changed. His way of life and testimony became such that those who rejected him before began to praise God for the great transformation that Paul had experienced.

When the Christian is truly born again, he always bears a good witness wherever he goes. He is the good perfume of Christ, which exudes the likeness of God (2 Cor 2:15). He does not need to strive to be honest, fair, pure, and respectful. This will flow naturally from his life, as someone who has been and continues to be transformed by the power of the Lord Jesus Christ.

Allow me to confront you, dear reader: Are you regenerated? Are you saved? Has your life been completely transformed by the work of God's grace and glory, so that your great joy is to love God and your neighbor with all your might?

Does your testimony, before the family of faith and those from outside confirm the Christianity that your lips speak of so much? If not, here is the sermon of the greatest preacher, with the greatest message (the gospel), calling you to repentance and faith, so that you may be saved!

CHAPTER 2

The Beatitudes

In the previous chapter we looked at the general context of the Sermon of the Mount. In this chapter we will overview the important topics of the Beatitudes before we dive deeper into them individually.

The Beatitudes are found in the first part of Jesus's Sermon on the Mount passage, in Matthew 5:3–12:

Blessed are the poor in spirit, for theirs is the kingdom of heaven.

Blessed are they that mourn: for they shall be comforted.

Blessed are the meek: for they shall inherit the earth.

Blessed are they which do hunger and thirst after righteousness: for they shall be filled.

Blessed are the merciful: for they shall obtain mercy.

Blessed are the pure in heart: for they shall see God.

Blessed are the peacemakers: for they shall be called the children of God.

Blessed are they which are persecuted for righteousness' sake: for theirs is the kingdom of heaven.

Blessed are ye, when men shall revile you, and persecute you, and shall say all manner of evil against you falsely, for my sake.

Rejoice, and be exceeding glad: for great is your reward in heaven: for so persecuted they the prophets which were before you.

The goal that remains in studying each of the Beatitudes is to draw as close as we can to the character of the true Christian, which is simply the expected conduct of God's people and their internal motivations and values. We will find that as we draw closer to that understanding, we will also understand better the Beatitudes.

What are the Beatitudes?

When Jesus began preaching the Sermon on the Mount, he used the expression "blessed." What does blessed mean? What are the "Beatitudes"? Blessed can be interpreted as any of the following: "happy," "blissful," "full," "complete," "satisfied," and even "more than happy."

In this passage, Jesus demonstrates that there is true happiness which is possible to obtain even while living in this fallen world. How, though, can happiness be found? It is only through the gospel, of being in Christ, that it can be enjoyed. Jesus taught that anyone who lives the life of the "blessed"—the poor, those who mourn, those who hunger and thirst for righteousness, the merciful, the clean of heart, the peacemaker, the persecuted for the sake of righteousness—is in fact happy, fortunate, and complete.

The way to true happiness

Throughout history, many have sought the secret to completely satisfaction, contentment, and happiness in life. Who does not wish to walk along a path filled with happiness? We as mankind all seek and yearn for inner peace; people from all walks of life want to be full, satisfied, and happy—fulfilled in this life.

Why is there so much unhappiness in the world? Why do men and women struggle to feel accomplished or complete, settled in discontentment? Understanding a little of the biblical doctrine of human creation helps us in this regard.

God perfectly made the universe, without any defect or failure. As reported in Genesis 1 and 2, the last work of Creation was the human being, created in the image and likeness of God (Gen 1:26). Because God created mankind male and female, in his image and likeness, they are endowed with qualities similar to those of God.

The qualities that God possesses are his attributes—characteristics that allow us to know who God is and what he does. Many of these attributes of God cannot be transmitted, as they are possessed only by him and cannot be shared by his creatures. Some of those attributes are omnipotence (the quality of having all power); omniscience (the quality of having all wisdom); and omnipresence (the quality of being everywhere, all the time).

In addition to the attributes that only God possesses, there are the communicable attributes that he shares to some extent with humanity, making them similar to him in these aspects. Some of these attributes includegoodness, justice, love, wisdom, and holiness. These attributes were granted to man at the moment of their creation.

Why is this important to remember? Because God is the ultimate, fulfilled, perfect, and completely happy Being. There is no sadness or emptiness in God. So, when God created man, he made him happy. The human being, before the Fall, had no need of anything, but was perfectly complete in God.

Genesis 2:8 describes man living in a place called the garden of Eden. The word "Eden" in Hebrew means a place of pleasure, a place of satisfaction. Man, therefore, was a complete being, who lived in a place full of pleasure and satisfaction. However, while Adam and Eve dwelt in the garden of Eden, Satan tempted Eve, enticing her to eat the fruit of the tree of knowledge of good and evil (Gen 3).

Satan's argument was, in essence, that if the woman ate the fruit forbidden by God, she and her husband would be happier, more complete than they were in obedience to him! The devil's plan was to tempt man to disobey God's order so that he could obtain a higher level of satisfaction and happiness. Satan's great offer was for man to be happy alone, in the freedom of disobedience to the Lord.

Unfortunately, Adam and Eve accepted Satan's suggestion and fell into sin, turning away from obedience to the Lord, thereby receiving the consequences of emptiness, guilt, and sadness. Their sin caused the world to be ruled by pain, hatred, violence, death, suicide, murder, depression, and anxiety.

The fall of man into sin teaches us a terrible lesson: if we stop obeying the Word of God—if we turn away from his ways, if we seek happiness outside of what is found in the Bible—we will be the most miserable of all men. Although Satan's enticements are real and appear to be advantageous when he implies, "Touch that woman," "go out with that young man," "drink that alcoholic beverage," the result of these acts will make us guilty, unhappy, and frustrated people.

Outside of the obedience to Christ, man is a monster, an uncontrolled animal struggling to satisfy his desires, displeasing God, hurting himself and hurting others around him. Sin steals man's happiness.

Unfortunately, because of the sin of Adam and Eve in the garden, people continue to seek happiness through personal satisfaction, apart from God: whether it is by alcohol or drugs, through success or fame, or by seeking beauty and all kinds of sexual pleasures. Some seek pleasure in buying things, greedily obtaining profit, and landing great achievements. Others live their whole lives planning trips and constantly entertaining themselves.

What did Jesus teach in the Beatitudes? He taught that even in a fallen world, there is the possibility of experiencing true happiness. There is the possibility of being complete and joyful in the midst of the darkness of the world, for the one who—through repentance and faith—enters the kingdom of God.

When the Lord Jesus went up that mount and preached the sermon, he was (and is!) presenting the kingdom of God to thousands who are empty, unhappy, depressed, suicidal, adulterous, drunken, and drug-addicted; he says, "You can be complete, and you can fully satisfy yourself by believing in the gospel and entering into my kingdom. You can be transformed into a blessed and happy people, receiving the grace of God."

Psalm 16:11b says, "In thy presence is fulness of joy; at thy right hand there are pleasures for evermore." What are "joy" and "pleasures"? This is true and ultimate happiness, completeness, and satisfaction; these terms depict joy, rejoicing, and jubilation. The Psalmist said it was in God's presence that he found true joy and pleasures. Only in the presence of God, in fellowship with Christ, will you find happiness.

The Psalmist continues with a similar statement in Psalm 84:10: "For a day in thy courts is better than a thousand. I had rather be a doorkeeper in the house of my God, than to dwell in the tents of wickedness." He would prefer only one day, full of joy, happiness, and grace in the presence of God than many other days in the so-called delights of sin. Once again the truth that happiness is only found in God is confirmed in Scripture.

I remember a testimony given by Pastor David Wilkerson (1931–2011) when he was on a radio show in New York along with a celebrity. After that star talked a lot about the pleasures he had already enjoyed and how he was in his ninth marriage, David Wilkerson quietly commented that he was in front of America's most unfortunate and empty man. This statement shocked the man, making him realize after speaking with the pastor that his whole life of pleasure would never complete him, because he had ignored Christ and the gospel.

The world teaches that the standard of happiness is based on possession of goods, objects, pleasures, and sensations. This is false happiness, a false completeness. The teaching of the fallen world is that to be happy, a poor man has to be rich; someone who is walking needs to have a car; someone who is sick needs to have good health, a man who is single has to have a wife; and someone who is married needs to have an extra-marital relationship.

If that argument and logic were correct, those who who have it all—great riches, fancy cars, perfect health and relationships—would be happy; yet they are not! They may even look happy for a while, but their happiness will not last until the next lust appears and they feel frustrated once again! Luke 12:15b clearly teaches: "for a man's life consisteth not in the abundance of the things which he possesseth." Even in the sinful state in which mankind exists, it is possible to find true happiness, regardless of how much physical or emotional pain plagues this world today.

A few years ago, I visited a woman who was at an advanced age (more than eighty years old). She couldn't walk, she was poor, surviving only on a small pension, and she was also restricted to the wheelchair she used daily. The daughter of that lady told me, "Make friends with her, because during the night she does not sleep. She spends the night praying. She can pray every night for you!" What a happy, blissful woman, full of life despite her physical condition. Why is that? She was saved by the gospel, had the truth, and was full of God's grace!

What about Mary Jane Taylor (1837–1870), wife of the English missionary Hudson Taylor (1832–1905), who lived in China? When she was dying in her poor house laying on a precarious bed, she said, "Dear Hudson, there has never been, throughout my life, even one cloud between my Savior and me." She died happy, fulfilled, and complete in her Lord.

In 2010, astonishing news was circulating in Brazil. Two pastors from the state of the Espírito Santo who were on the way to a ministerial meeting in their church were involved in a tragic accident with seven other vehicles. The car they were in was crushed between two trucks, trapping the pastors in the wreckage. When the fire department rescue team arrived, they tried to get the men out because they were losing blood quickly.

While the first responders tried to reach them in the midst of the twisted wreckage, the pastors began to sing out loud, "Nearer my God to Thee, nearer to Thee. E'en though it be a cross that raiseth me." Little by little their voices faded, and with their death came complete silence. The people who were rescuing them were so impacted by the calm, sweet confidence the two men demonstrated in death, that they had to stop, stunned and unable to move.

Why did those men die peacefully singing? Because they trusted the Lord completely; they had their lives securely placed in the hands of their precious Savior, and they were happy, blissful, and blessed.

However painful the way of the Beatitudes may seem to the world, for the one who is saved—who has God as the greatest treasure and whose hope is in the world to come—the Beatitudes are the way of blessing and fulfillment. They communicate to the saints the foreseen joys of eternity!

Thus, with the Beatitudes, Jesus was pointing out that the way to a life of full satisfaction cannot be known in the delight of sin, filling yourself with the things of this world. Being blessed is knowing and being transformed by the gospel. Only the Word of God, which reveals the gospel of God's grace and glory, can grant true freedom and happiness to anyone. Happiness, therefore, is only for the one who believes in the gospel and has in his life the qualities that Jesus pointed out in the Beatitudes.

The marks of the true Christian

The Beatitudes, in addition to being the way to true happiness, point to the characteristics expected by God in every true Christian. There is no way of being part of God's own people if one does not possess and progressively develop each one of the Beatitudes more and more. As previously mentioned, Matthew 5:13 teaches that salt is not truly salt if it is not composed of the qualities which make it salt. Jesus concludes that the characteristics of the true Christian are like salt: it gives flavor to the food, it does not suffer corruption and, moreover, it prevents the degradation of the food in which it is placed. Just as salt has distinct qualities, the true Christian has well-defined properties.

Are you a true Christian? Are you genuinely converted? Are you saved, without the condemnation of sin weighing you down? If the salvation of God is a reality in your life, then you are poor in spirit, you weep, you are meek, you hunger and thirst for righteousness, you are merciful, you are clean of heart, you are a peacemaker, you are persecuted and you suffer because of His holy name. These are the marks of the true Christian, the true salt of God.

They are not just characteristics of the patriarchs and prophets of the Old Testament, of the apostles, or of the men and women of God in the past. They are not only expected of pastors, deacons, or missionaries. The Sermon on the Mount states that they are the marks of every true Christian. Every one of God's people—man or woman, young or old—needs to possess and grow in these qualities daily.

The Beatitudes, in addition to being the marks of all genuine Christians, must each be present in every Christian. You cannot be only merciful, without a portion of poverty of spirit or being clean of heart. In every Christian, there will always be each one of the Beatitudes, even if their prominence is marked by a greater intensity from one time to another.

However, if there are no such marks on someone who says he is a Christian, Jesus made the severe warning, "It is thenceforth good for nothing, but to be cast out, and to be trodden under foot of men" (Matt 5:13b). Someone without the properties of the saved—the Beatitudes—does not have the hope of eternal life, but rather the grim expectation of the coming judgment and eternal condemnation. Jesus was categorical in concluding the Beatitudes, showing that only those who possess them are, in fact, the justified and pure people of God.

Matthew 5:20 says, "For I say unto you, that except your righteousness shall exceed the righteousness of the scribes and Pharisees, ye shall in no case enter into the kingdom of heaven." This verse can be read as follows, "If your righteousness, conduct, and standards are not above that practiced by the Pharisees and Scribes, you cannot be saved." The Scribes and Pharisees did not enter the kingdom of God, for they were not salt. Their legalism, hypocrisy, carnality, and pride were only covered by a "religious cloak," but inside these people were corrupt and evil, so that Jesus called them white-washed sepulchers (Matt 23:27).

Jesus said that the Scribes and Pharisees were not transformed, they did not receive a new heart, and they had not experienced the new birth and conversion. All they had was external righteousness, a religious habit, but it was not true religion, that which would have changed their character and made them new creatures.

How can the righteousness of the Scribes and Pharisees be overcome? Are you now meek? Is your heart clean and pure? Do you hear the Word of God and practice it, like the prudent man who built his house upon the rock (Matt 7:24–25)? If this is true about you, then your righteousness is exceeding that of the Scribes and Pharisees!

Do you have hunger and thirst for God? Do you mortify sin, fighting actively not to covet a man or woman in your heart (Matt 5:27–30)? You see, your righteousness is exceeding that of the Scribes and Pharisees!

Matthew 6:33 is the great mark of the true Christian: "But seek first the kingdom of God, and his righteousness; and all these things shall be added unto you." Are you saved? If so, God's will occupies the first place in your life. Every true Christian works, studies, buys and sells, travels—that is, they live as a normal citizen in this world; however, in all things, their priority is to do God's will. For the Christian, God's Word should have preeminence in all that he does, whether in thought or in deed.

Putting it in practical terms, the true Christian does not give as a daily tribute to the Lord a superficial, cold, and disinterested prayer; he does not read the Scriptures irreverently or in haste; he does not live all day in sin against God and his neighbor, coveting, being proud, being stingy; he does not speak in a disingenuous way that only offers lip service to God.

Blessed Christians live every moment of their days giving honor and glory to God. They live in a spirit of prayer, meditating on the holy Scripture of God, deviating from evil, and when they sin, they grieve and subsequently confess the sin to God whom they love so much and do not want to offend!

The only way of life that pleases God is the one lived according to the Beatitudes. The possession and practice of these characteristics pleases the Lord of heaven and earth, for it is the reflection of the life that his Son Jesus lived while in this world.

Is there in your heart a sincere desire to please and give joy to God? Then you must be transformed by the gospel of God's grace and continue along the path of the sanctification to become even more meek, humble, merciful—to become more and more Christlike. The more like Jesus Christ your life is, the more the Father will be pleased with you. This does not mean that God ultimately accepts us based on our works, but it means that, for love, you will make your salvation even firmer before the blessed Lord (2 Pet 1:10, 1 Cor 9:24–27).

Perhaps someone says that they have an affinity for biblical Christianity, but if the fruits produced by that person are not in accordance with the Beatitudes, there is no saving faith in them. Matthew 7:20 made it clear that the evidence of salvation is the accompanying fruit: "by their fruits ye shall know them." James 2:26b complements: "faith without works is dead."

Therefore, through the fruits—the evidences of faith—we can know if someone is converted. Without the will and practice of the Beatitudes in the life of a person, there is no true salvation.

Another fundamental characteristic in the life of a true Christian is their love and obedient zeal for the Word of God. See the Old Testament teaching on this theme in Psalm 1:1–3,

> Blessed is the man that walketh not in the counsel of the ungodly, nor standeth in the way of sinners, nor sitteth in the seat of the scornful. But his delight is in the law of the LORD; and in his law doth he meditate day and night. And he shall be like a tree planted by the rivers of water, that bringeth forth his fruit in his season; his leaf also shall not wither; and whatsoever he doeth shall prosper.

Now see what the New Testament says in James 1:25, "But whoso looketh into the perfect law of liberty, and continueth therein, he being not a forgetful hearer, but a doer of the work, this man shall be blessed in his deed."

Who are the blessed? Those who have been regenerated by God, who are pleased with the Law of the Lord, who know it deeply, who walk with the God of the Bible, who have a life of prayer, who fast to the Lord in secret, who are sanctified day by day, who go to the house of God. The one who is happy and complete, lacking nothing, is faithful and holy!

Would this not be the time for us to eat and drink until we are satisfied with pure heavenly food? Would this not be the generation of Christians who need to be sanctified and made in the likeness of Christ? Are we not the church of Christ on earth, who urgently needs a powerful and effective testimony to fight the dense darkness that surrounds us?

It is time to love and walk in close fellowship with the God of Scripture! See the invitation of Jesus, that we may nourish ourselves in him from John 6:35: "I am the bread of life: he that cometh to me shall never hunger; and he that believeth on me shall never thirst."

We are bloated and unsatisfied by the "bread of the earth." We are intoxicated with this world and its system. We have so much sophistication, so much technology and electronics, so many social networks and virtual environments; all of this is causing exactly what Jesus said in John 6.49, "Your fathers did eat manna in the wilderness and are dead." How many today are walking around as living dead, missing the vibrancy and vitality of the Christian life, because they eat only the "bread of the earth" instead of the bread of heaven?

Dear reader, the Beatitudes show us that the character of the true Christian appears the more they walk with their God, the more they are filled with his Word, the more they spend time with him in prayer and regular meditation, and the more they have fellowship with the Lord and obey him.

Warning against the deception of the world

There is one last aspect to be analyzed, before we leave this introduction to the Beatitudes and study each of them individually.

We live in times of great changes in values, in which the truth has became negotiable and completely relativized. The postmodern mindset accepts no limits. Our Western society is already considered a post-truth society, in which the absolute truth is no longer important. Truth is sacrificed at the altar of personal satisfaction and enjoyment.

Even so, with this so-called freedom, never before have we seen society with the greatest existential vacuum. There are multitudes of children without the care of their parents, young people without perspective, ruined couples, and the elderly being led to forgetfulness. I believe that this last aspect of the Beatitudes provides an answer to the worldly system that governs our time.

The Beatitudes teach how misleading the appearance of this world can be. Since the Fall of our first parents in Eden, Satan has promised to his victims happiness and completeness in rebellion and disobedience to God (as we have seen above). The Beatitudes show that this strategy is completely false and cannot guarantee real satisfaction to anyone. The Beatitudes destroy the illusion of the pleasures of this world, they end the intoxication that the world brings, breaking down the popularity of the works of the flesh to obtain pleasure and peace.

When Jesus preached the Beatitudes, the only means he said that could satisfy the human being fully was diametrically opposed to the means propagated by the corrupt worldly system. While the world offers fulfillment for the rich, young, and beautiful, those who take in sin in long "gulps" and amass possessions and properties and fame, Jesus said that happy are those who weep, are poor, and hunger and thirst for justice. Happy are the clean of heart, and happy are the peacemakers!

In Scripture, King Solomon possessed an extraordinary abundance of all that the world believed to bring happiness. First Kings 10–11 shows that his wealth was incomparable, even to the highest current standards. Solomon was the richest man on earth. In his time, there was so much gold in Israel that silver was considered to be worthless. Imagine, so much gold that silver has become something insignificant and negligible!

As a king, he ruled the empire of Israel in its golden age, when he had his largest geographic extent. No other king of Israel achieved as much power as he did. He was David's son, belonged to the Messianic lineage, and was a descendant of the patriarchs Abraham, Isaac, and Jacob.

Solomon was married to seven hundred women who were among the most beautiful in the world at the time, all of them princesses. In addition, he had a private harem with three hundred concubines, who were readily available when called upon. If Solomon slept with a different woman every night, it would take more than two and a half years to see the same woman again!

In properties and architecture, his reign was incomparable. His agricultural techniques had the best technology of that time; his vineyards and wheat plantations grew every year. His palace and royal mansions left visitors from other nations amazed. He owned a fleet of international ships and alliances that guaranteed him an annual supply of the most precious, exotic, and refined things the world has ever known!

In the field of knowledge, there was no one who could outweigh him in wisdom and skill. Solomon was endowed with a rich, vast, detailed, and poetic mind, millimetrically built to ensure a reasoning that made the great wise men of the east look like boys in grade school compared to him.

What was Solomon's conclusion about happiness that the world offered him when he composed his last book: "Vanity of vanities, saith the Preacher, vanity of vanities; all is vanity" (Eccl 1:2). It was as if he had said: "It was all in vain. I chased after the wind. What I thought would bring me joy was actually the greatest delusion of my life." He finished his career in this world sad and oppressed by the many sins he had committed.

Dear reader, there's still time for you! There is still hope for a real change in your life, which will lead you to true, long-lasting and immortal happiness!

Listen to Jesus's invitation to you and to the whole world, "Come unto me, all ye that labour and are heavy laden, and I will give you rest" (Matt 11:28). Find your rest, peace, fullness, and complete joy in Christ!

It does not matter what you've been doing or who you are. It does not matter if you are a scoundrel who has lived the most sordid experiences in the black dungeons of sin. It doesn't matter if you are an unbeliever, confused, thinking of abandoning everything; perhaps you have lost all sense of day and night, cold and hot, right and wrong; it doesn't matter if you are bewildered, depressed and sad. No matter your past, Jesus is calling you exactly as you are today. Come to him, immerse yourself in his love and forgiveness, so that Christ may give you new life, new hope and may put in you his Beatitudes. If you really want true joy, satisfaction, and happiness, do not despise God's goodness and mercy. He promised that he would welcome you and would not cast you out (John 6:37).

CHAPTER 3

Blessed Are the Poor in Spirit

The great goal in our study of the Beatitudes is to trace the character of the true Christian. The first aspect of this Christian model was taught by Jesus in Matthew 5:3, "Blessed are the poor in spirit: for theirs is the kingdom of heaven."

Before we point out the definition and the characteristics of the poor in spirit, let's look at its counterpart. Caution is needed in explaining this quality so that we do not create an incorrect image of what our Lord meant with humility/poverty of spirit.

False Perceptions of "The Poor in Spirit"

By reading this verse, we can quickly conclude that Jesus might be referring to all miserable people as being heirs of the kingdom of God. Many people think that being financially poor with poor living conditions is a marker of great spirituality and citizenship of heaven. However, with a closer look at the doctrine of all Scripture, we can see that Christ is not speaking of material poverty.

If we examine church history, we will see that in the 4th century, the Roman Emperor Constantine (274–337) supposedly converted to Christianity, giving great freedom to the church, until he was persecuted and martyred. Little by little, with the influence of that emperor, the church began to adopt Greco-Roman elements in its services, marring their practice of Christian living and moving away from the teaching of the Bible.

People who were concerned about sin being institutionalized in the church began to abandon it, beginning a movement of lonely pilgrims who sought isolation in deserts, caves, and forests. This was the beginning of the monastic movement, in which the idea of salvation began to be associated with the life of deprivation and poverty. It was widely taught that God did not like rich people and wealth—that the person, to be holy, would need to be poor, for only then could they inherit eternal life.

However, this cannot be the correct interpretation, because if it were so all the poor would go directly to heaven and all the rich would go directly to hell, due to their respective natures. We know that neither of the two alternatives is true, because the New Testament bears witness that people who were financially poor were saved (Luke 16:19–31) and also the rich (Matt 27:57–60).

Financial or social misery is not a guarantee of spirituality to anyone, because experience shows that there are many poor people who are petty and greedy and love the little money they have; while there are very rich people who are pious and have no love for money.

Scripture states that both wealth and poverty are conditions that come from God and fulfill his purposes in the world: "The rich and poor meet together: the LORD is the maker of them all" (Prov 22:2). Therefore, neither poverty nor wealth guarantee spirituality to any person.

If physical poverty were synonymous with spirituality and salvation, the Lord Jesus would have done great evil to many people because he took away the poverty of many. How many hungry people did he feed? How many blind people, paralytics, and lepers did he heal, giving them the opportunity to return to a status of employment? If physical poverty created salvation in itself, Jesus should have left all these people in misery, so as not to compromise their eternity! Those who think that the humility/poverty referred to in this verse concerns a person's material lack are mistaken.

Secondly, Jesus's teaching on being poor in spirit does not refer to spiritual poverty. There are people who think that being poor in spirit means someone being poor in loving, in praying, in knowledge of Scripture, and in sanctification. They think that the man who is spiritually malnourished, breaking fasts, with no commitment to public service, and putting the gospel in a bad light before society is poor in spirit. No, this cannot be a blessed person, the poor of spirit.

Thirdly, there are those who think that because they do not have a spiritual leadership role in the kingdom of God, such as a pastor, deacon, or other ministers, they can be considered poor in spirit due to their failed devotion to the Lord. Such thought is nothing more than a license for carnality, a subterfuge for many to continue living in open sin against God.

All Christians, absolutely all, are called to have life in abundance through Jesus Christ (John 10:10). All who are called are also trained and exhorted by the Lord of heaven to meditate day and night on the Scriptures (Ps 1:2), pray in secret, without ceasing, and publicly (Matt 6:6, 1 Thess 5:17, 1 Tim 2:8), preach in time and out of time (2 Tim 4:2), and avoid drunkenness with wine, rather be filled with the Holy Spirit (Eph 5:18).

Therefore, Jesus was not saying that poverty of spirit would correspond to having a poor spiritual life. On the contrary, the Christian is called to be full of all the fullness of God's knowledge; the believer is called to be full of the power of the Holy Spirit, to bear much fruit and to proclaim to all whom he knows of his Lord.

Finally, being poor in spirit has no relation to self-pity. A common mistake in interpreting this passage is to imagine that people who practice self-pity, who have low esteem, who consider themselves as a "poor thing," miserable, weak, sinful, who continually refer to themselves as stupid—they fulfill the requirement of being poor in spirit as taught in this beatitude. This is not the type of person to whom Jesus is referring here, because this attitude of self-pity is sin before God's eyes. It is nothing more than false spirituality and the proud desire to demonstrate to other men a false pity (see Matt 6:16).

The person who acts like this may really be small and poor in words and actions before other people, however, do this test: mess with their vanities, mess with their ego, treat them as the worst of all creatures, rebuke them for some sin, or correct them in some fault in the presence of other people. You will see that the one who called himself such a sinner will resent himself fiercely rather than admonish you (see the Pharisees and Jesus, Matt 21). At the very heart of these people there is arrogance and a vain heart, which has nothing to do with the poor in spirit of whom Jesus is teaching.

Thus, poverty of spirit does not mean anyone who depreciates themselves with words, but then, upon confrontation, deny with their words and actions everything they said with their lips.

True Nature of "The Poor in Spirit"

After looking at four aspects of what it does not mean to be poor in spirit, let's take a look at the true nature of one who is poor in spirit. The character of the true Christian involves, necessarily, that they recognize not having any merit in themselves to be accepted or forgiven. Such a person recognizes the impossibility of salvation by any work of their own, only by the help of another—God. In simple terms, being poor in spirit means to be aware of your own spiritual misery; it is to be completely dependent on the grace, mercy, and love of God for your salvation.

How do you see if someone is poor? You identify a poor person through their presented needs. If the richest billionaire in the world were to be analyzed financially, what need could he or she possibly have? None! So, he or she could not be considered poor. However, when someone is analyzed and it is identified that there is a shortage in certain areas, they can be considered poor in whatever it is that is lacking. Therefore, the greater the need, the greater the level of poverty of that person.

In the New Testament there are two words for poverty. One of the terms used in Greek to define poor refers to that person who has no luxury, no comfort, no riches, but who has the basic needs. They do not go hungry and they do not experience great difficulty, but only have the basic essential to live. It is the type of person who cannot enjoy the good things or fulfill their own desires. For example, this word would represent those who cannot buy a car, have an annual holiday trip, or who cannot buy a house of their own, but can, however, live day to day with their basic needs met.

The second term for poor in the New Testament Greek is the same one used in the parable of the rich and the beggar, when Jesus described Lazarus as hungry, miserable, extremely poor, full of wounds, and completely lost. This is the same word used in the first beatitude we are analyzing, to mean that the happy, accomplished, and complete are those who see themselves as depraved and lacking in all spiritual help, insufficient for anything concerning God and his salvation.

By using this word for poverty of spirit, Jesus wanted his listeners to recognize their total dependence on God. They were completely incapable to meet the most basic of spiritual needs. They needed to understand themselves as spiritually ruined and broke, people who could not provide anything for themselves. They were people who had no merit that made them acceptable before God.

In this way, to be poor in spirit is to recognize that none of our works are accepted before the holy God; it is to recognize that everything we do in the eagerness to obtain salvation is nothing but filthy and unacceptable rags before the Lord; finally, it is to understand that nothing in us can impress, move, justify, or make us worthy in the presence of the Father. The poor in spirit are those who recognize themselves in this level of misery before God.

However, perhaps you ask yourself: where is the joy, blessedness, and happiness in this way of life? Jesus responds in the Sermon on the Mount with the first beatitude, "Happy is the man who comes to God humiliated and poor. Happy is the man who bends the knee, bows down and speaks as a beggar to God. Happy is the one who recognizes his state of smallness, of dependence on the Lord. This is blissful, blessed fullness, because he does not see his own merits, he does not trust in his talents, his eloquence, fortune, intelligence, family support, or his natural talents."

The poor in spirit can only see the cross of Calvary. In it lies all their hope and dependence. They can sing "Rock of Ages," along with the composer Augustus Toplady (1740–1778): "Nothing in my hand I bring, simply to the cross I cling."

Why was poverty of spirit placed as the foremost, the first of the Beatitudes? Because poverty of spirit is what allows a person to enjoy the other Beatitudes. Without being poor in spirit, someone cannot cry, cannot hunger and thirst for righteouness, cannot be clean of heart. Being poor in spirit is the gateway to the kingdom of God.

Biblical Examples of "The Poor in Spirit"

Later in the gospel of Matthew, Jesus said, "Neither do men put new wine into old bottles; else the bottles break, and the wine runneth out, and the bottles perish: but they put new wine into new bottles, and both are preserved" (Matt 9:17). To be filled with the kingdom of God, first one needs to purge themselves of the old man, emptying themselves of vanity, greed, passion for the world, and pride. Once empty of the "old wine," through a humble spirit—in this poor state of spirit we've been examining—one can then be filled with the "new wine" of the Beatitudes, which characterize the Christian.

The biblical comparison between someone who is poor in spirit and someone who is not, is found in the parable of the Pharisee and the publican, in Luke 18:9–14,

> And he spake this parable unto certain which trusted in themselves that they were righteous,and despised others: two men went up into the temple to pray; the one a Pharisee, and the other a publican. The Pharisee stood and prayed thus with himself, God, I thank thee, that I am not as other men are, extortioners, unjust, adulterers, or even as this publican. I fast twice in the week, I give tithes of all that I possess. And the publican, standing afar off, would not lift up so much as his eyes unto heaven, but smote upon his breast, saying, God be merciful to me a sinner! I tell you, this man went down to his house justified rather than the other: for every one that exalteth himself shall be abased; and he that humbleth himself shall be exalted.

The biggest of the obstacles for someone to be in fact poor in spirit is self-righteousness. It denotes the willingness to justify ourselves, to choose what should and should not be obeyed in the Word of God according to our preferences and also, to be indulgent with our own lives to the extent that we do not consider ourselves to be lost sinners—or perhaps not that lost.

The Pharisee of the parable above is the portrait of those who are not poor in spirit. His long and pompous prayer was full of haughtiness, pride, and self-righteousness. He prayed, not to obtain the favor of the holy majesty of God, but to show his alleged righteousness to the Lord. It was as if he were praying to himself, to be self-satisfied with his performance and conduct. Access to the Father is strictly forbidden by someone who goes to him in this way. As said in verse 14, the Pharisee went down from the temple of God still burdened by his sins, with the righteous wrath and condemnation of God hovering over his head. He was not—and could never have been—justified by the Lord unless he had recognized his personal poorness.

Now, let us see the publican in his prayer to God. He almost did not speak. His body posture was so discrete as was the inner contrition of his heart; he was beating his breast, as if externally showing the abomination he was in his own eyes. He didn't dare look up or speak many words in the presence of God—not because he did not have anything to say—but because he thought he was unworthy to refer to God by being who he was and doing what he did.

Look at the blessed: he thought he was unworthy to come in the presence of God, he had no selfish motivation to address God, and he felt small and despicable! With his speech he said, "I am no one, I have no dignity, I have no rights and merits, I have no justice to present to you, Oh God!"

It is interesting to note that this was exactly the position of the two main Jewish leaders in the restoration of Jerusalem after the Babylonian captivity. If you could have found Ezra in life, you would have seen the noblest scribe and priest of his time—truly poor of spirit despite the position and capacity he had—praying thus,

> O my God! I am ashamed and blush to lift up my face to thee, my God: for our iniquities are increased over our head, and our trespass is grown up unto the heavens. . . . Oh! Lord God of Israel, thou art righteous: for we remain yet escaped, as it is this day: behold, we are before thee in our trespasses: for we cannot stand before thee because of this. (Ezra 9:6, 15)

See the supplication of Nehemiah, the friend of the king, nominated as the governor-general of Jerusalem—another genuine person poor of spirit,

> Let thine ear now be attentive, and thine eyes open, that thou mayest hear the prayer of thy servant, which I pray before thee now, day and night, for the children of Israel thy servants, and confess the sins of the children of Israel, which we have sinned against thee: both I and my father's house have sinned. We have dealt very corruptly against thee, and have not kept the commandments, nor the statutes, nor the judgments, which thou commandedst thy servant Moses. . . . Oh! Lord, I beseech thee, let now thine ear be attentive to the prayer of thy servant, and to the prayer of thy servants, who desire to fear thy name. (Neh 1:6–7, 11)

We see in Scripture that the Lord mightily used those who were poor in spirit, such as Nehemiah and Ezra. May we heed their examples.

Conclusion

Dear reader, I cannot close without asking you: who are you, the Pharisee or the sinner?

Is your prayer to God, if ever you have prayed, filled with justifications, not assuming responsibility and confessing your guilt? Do you make excuses for yourself and allow yourself to be who you are and do what you do before the righteous Lord? Do you calmly and coldly shrug your shoulders to proven facts to rid your consciousness of the voice of rebuke of the Holy Spirit? Then nothing else can be expected for you than the condemnation given to the Pharisee.

His righteousness does not come from God. His apparent wealth will become poverty on the day when God will judge the living and the dead. The apparent pity you show today will be broken when the Judge of the whole earth tests your life by fire. My plea is for you to repent immediately, crying out to God for forgiveness and mercy.

However, you may have identified with the above exposure regarding the publican. It is possible that, while reading, you were cut to heart, broken and contrite by recognizing in the publican what is true about you! Did this story describe something that is a reality in your life today? Are you the one who prays, "God, if the Lord wants to send me to hell now, the Lord will have committed the greatest act of justice, for it is all that I deserve. However, I cry out for your mercy and kindness"?

If that is true, trust you are blessed. The spirit of the glory and grace of God rests on you. Every accusation and condemnation has gone, you have gone from death to life and are declared innocent, justified before God. Be happy, joyful, and blessed!

Jesus promised the reward to those who are poor in spirit: "Of him is the kingdom of heaven." It is as if he had said, "This one will not see the second death. He has been regenerated, and is saved. He will enter through the pearly gates of the New Jerusalem, to live forever in the fullest dawn." Are you poor in spirit? Then the kingdom of God, which was prepared before the foundation of the world, awaits your arrival.

CHAPTER 4

Blessed Are Those Who Mourn

The Sermon on the Mount continues with Jesus's teaching of a very interesting characteristic of the true Christian in Matthew 5:4, "Blessed are they that mourn: for they shall be comforted."

When we read Jesus's words here, they seem quite at odds: are those who weep happy? How can that be? How can joy and sadness, happiness and pain, scourge and love, be united to make someone complete, if they are so opposite in nature?

With this statement of the Lord we are introduced, intentionally, to a paradox. A paradox occurs when two truths contradict each other—two things that are equally true but oppose each other. Why does Jesus say happy are those who weep or mourn? How does we reconcile these ideas?

The world with its system of values considers this idea simply ridiculous, pathetic, and unsustainable. In the eyes of the wicked it seems more like the whim of a selfish and tyrant God, who does not want the happiness of his creatures. Blessedness for the secular system is a continuous fight not to lose, not to cry, not to be in any way disadvantaged. That is why the world's largest industry is the one that promotes leisure, entertainment, parties, enjoyment, and pleasure. Those who live this beatitude—that in which happiness comes from the righteous cry and those who weep are blessed—are repudiated by the world and exist in stark contrast with the corrupt and sinful system that operates in the children of disobedience.

False Perception of Those Who Mourn

Before we continue to define what Jesus speaks of by "crying," it must be pointed out that many people around the world cry copiously every day. Is every person who cries a blessed person? Will any kind of weeping receive the consolation promised by Jesus?

We need to remember that the Beatitudes are not natural qualities of the flesh. What Jesus said in the second beatitude was not about the cries of all people in general. The fallen human nature cannot produce the Beatitudes, because they are spiritual qualities, so the mourning referred to by Jesus is something that is spiritually generated. It is necessary to have this in mind, because many people around the world use this passage to console the multitudes that weep, saying, "See my daughter, because you are weeping, be sure that Jesus will console you, for he promised to console all those who weep."

The mourning Jesus addressed in this text is not that of a woman who was abandoned by her husband, or of some mother in the slum who had her children imprisoned because of drug trafficking; it is not of the father who could not buy a present for his son, or of a housewife who lost her son in a tragic accident; it is not the cry of the unemployed person or of those who have had a failed relationship; it is not the pain of verbal aggression or of victims of atrocious crimes; it is not crying for the painful diseases that afflict someone's body or mind; it is not the cry of the financial crisis and the bankruptcy of a company or the cry of shame and humiliation; it is not the case, either, of the agonizing cries of the depressed, immersed in melancholy and despair.

All these situations, without doubt, produce sadness, unrest and profound affliction, but they are not the ones who have received God's promise of consolation. If these "cries" were those Jesus had in mind when he stated this beatitude, almost all the world's people would receive the consolation promised by the Lord; however we know that to not be the case.

There are clear examples of cries and sorrows in the Bible that also went without consolation. Look at Cain's case, after cold-bloodedly and cruelly assassinating his brother Abel in Genesis 4:13–14: "And Cain said unto the LORD, My punishment is greater than I can bear. Behold, thou hast driven me out this day from the face of the earth; and from thy face shall I be hid; and I shall be a fugitive and a vagabond in the earth; and it shall come to pass, that every one that findeth me shall slay me." Cain realized the gravity of the judgment that he would receive for his barbaric act, causing him to feel great fear for his life, but that is not the sadness that Jesus was saying about "those who weep."

Esau, Jacob's brother, wept after realizing that he had lost his birthright and the blessings of his father Jacob, but this sadness did not restore to him the lost promise or the covenant with God (Gen 27:30–38, Heb 12:16–17).

The wicked king of Israel, Ahab, when he failed in the desire to possess a vineyard, he was heavy and displeased, because his greed and avarice could not be immediately satisfied (1 Kgs 21:1–5). Beware, because the crying for failing to make profits or for the loss of personal belongings has already led many—including Ahab himself—to disgrace in life and eternal ruin (1 Kgs 21:7–19, 1 Tim 6).

What about Judas Iscariot, the traitor of the Lord Jesus? Matthew 27:1–5 tells of his betrayal, remorse, and suicide:

When the morning was come, all the chief priests and elders of the people took counsel against Jesus to put him to death: And when they had bound him, they led him away, and delivered him to Pontius Pilate the governor. Then Judas, which had betrayed him, when he saw that he was condemned, repented himself, and brought again the thirty pieces of silver to the chief priests and elders, Saying, I have sinned in that I have betrayed the innocent blood. And they said, What is that to us? See thou to that. And he cast down the pieces of silver in the temple, and departed, and went and hanged himself.

After seeing the end result of his actions, Judas was troubled, yet nothing that he came to do would change the horrible consequence and judgment he would receive for his act. He actually wept, but God no longer heard him. He was taken by pain and misery, but there was no one to console him. The time had passed for consolation (Jer 8:20).

Let us always remember these solemn examples, to remind us that many have wept, weep, and will weep, but not all will be comforted. One is mistaken to think that by the simple fact of crying and grieving one can receive the relief of the promise contained in the second beatitude.

True Nature of Those Who Mourn

If it is not just any person's mourning that will receive the divine consolation—what kind of mourning is it? The Greek word recorded by Matthew as weeping in this passage occurs only a few times in the New Testament; it means praying, mourning, a deep and painful lament, it is a crying accompanied by agony and pain in your heart, as the weeping following the death of a loved one. This word refers to someone taken aback by such sadness to the point that it cannot be contained; it speaks of a pain that cannot be hidden or suppressed.

The cry that Jesus speaks of is a blessed cry provoked only in the one born again by the Holy Spirit. Only the one who has received a new heart and mind, by the grace of God, can manifest this sorrow for their own sin and for the sinfulness that exists in the world. This quality of crying, therefore, is produced by the Spirit of God.

How do you know that a person has been regenerated? One way is to see their sensitivity to sin. They will not stop sinning or be perfect on this earth, but their conscience will be greatly affected each time they sin, bringing about repentance and their abandonment of and disgust with everything that offends God. Such a person is not indifferent, self-indulgent, or insensitive, but is someone marked by spiritual discernment and aversion to sin.

That is why one of the evidences of true Christian character is to weep. Genuine Christians cannot contain themselves, cannot hide what their minds thought, their hands touched, or their lips kissed. They cannot declare, in any case, peace and forgiveness to thoughts and acts that Yahweh abhors. They are sensitive to every form of scandal against God and his holy Word, so that committing sin and not giving the glory due to God is the great sorrow of their sincere and repentant hearts.

Luke recorded the character of a woman who represents the cry of the blessed in Luke 7:36–38, "[Jesus] went into the Pharisee's house, and sat down to meat. And, behold, a woman in the city, which was a sinner, when she knew that Jesus sat at meat in the Pharisee's house, brought an alabaster box of ointment, and stood at his feet behind him weeping, and began to wash his feet with tears, and did wipe them with the hairs of her head, and kissed his feet, and anointed them with the ointment."

The woman reported here was a sinner, probably a prostitute. When she had the opportunity to enter the same enclosure that Jesus was in, the first thing she did was to humble herself at the feet of Jesus, crying abundantly in sincere repentance. She wept so much that her tears were enough to wash the Master's feet.

The context of the whole passage shows that the woman was convinced of her sins, feeling the burden and pressure of her transgressions, recognizing that if there was someone who could help her in her agony it would be the God-Man before whom she was prostrated. The woman knew that her life and acts were an offense to the holy God. She felt the depth of her perdition. It was as if she had said while weeping, "I have sinned, I committed adultery, I have committed prostitution, Lord. But I repent, I repent, and I repent; have compassion on me, kind Savior!"

We know that this blessed prostitute obtained forgiveness and salvation, because of Christ's response to her, who said that her sins were forgiven by the saving faith she had demonstrated (Luke 7:48–50).

Another biblical example of repentance was the contrite cry of King David, after having committed adultery with Bathsheba and disloyally killing her husband Uriah (2 Sam 11). Some time later, Nathan the prophet was sent by God to the palace of David to expose his terrible sin.

As king, David could have denied the sin, presented excuses for it, put the blame on Bathsheba, or even have had Nathan the prophet arrested and killed. At most, in his humiliation, he could have heard Nathan's rebuke and spent a few days ashamed before the people, and then simply "forget it," pretending that everything was fine and continue to live his life peacefully.

Was that what the blessed mourner did? Not at all! On hearing Nathan's rebuke, David immediately confessed his sin (2 Sam 12:13). There was no word of justification. There was no fight, debate, or denial. Only the simple and direct confession of sin.

Where, then, does the cry of David appear? Psalm 51:1–4 records it:

Have mercy upon me, O God, according to thy lovingkindness: according unto the multitude of thy tender mercies blot out my transgressions. Wash me thoroughly from mine iniquity, and cleanse me from my sin. For I acknowledge my transgressions: and my sin is ever before me. Against thee, thee only, have I sinned, and done this evil in thy sight: that thou mightest be justified when thou speakest, and be clear when thou judgest.

Can you see David's cry upon recognizing that he offended the Lord? It was the weeping for having grieved the Holy Spirit; it was the weeping of having offended God's glory, it was the weeping for his own sin. David showed the example of how to weep for his own wickedness, imperfections, and weaknesses. He did not weep for anything else or for feeling that he was being wronged by the error of others. It was his sin which stained him, and made him look evil and dirty in God's eyes. David's sorrow and pain were due only to his shortcomings. He wept for his sins, for his debauchery, and for his iniquity. With his cry, he was admitting and confessing his own sin. The Apostle Paul demonstrated this same truth in Romans 7, when he spoke of his struggle to do the good that he consciously desired and the sadness when he fell, through weakness, into the sin against which he fought. He concluded his speech exclaiming, in Romans 7:24: "O wretched man that I am! Who shall deliver me from the body of this death?" He was feeling the weight of his misery and the burden of his sin; he was lamenting his own wickedness. That has always been the true mark of the one truly saved: sensitivity.

Let me ask you directly, dear reader: how long have you gone without mourning over your sin? I don't mean crying and asking for a wife or husband, a house, a car, a loan, or for healing. I want to know how long it has been since you cried for forgiveness, confessing your miseries, confessing the inherent wickedness of your mind and the darkest iniquities of your heart?

You can confess and not deny your sins; you can name them and say them out loud before God. Yet, is there sorrow for them in your heart, is there sincere repentance?

Are there still tears in your eyes due to the pain caused by offending the majesty of God? Do you feel your miseries, knowing the strength and weight of your sin? Blessed are those who weep and confess their evil doing at the foot of the cross, convinced of their own sins.

Perhaps you still ask yourself: why should I cry? Why should I humble myself and feel deep sorrow? Because if the Spirit of God truly dwells in your life, you have received a new nature, which gives you a new way of seeing life. He who was previously dominated by indifference and coldness, by the insatiable desire for pleasure and advantages at all costs, is now dominated by a new spiritual nature which is pure, compassionate, and just.

Someone who possesses this new nature cannot keep back the tears. This is what 1 John 1:8–9 teaches, "If we say that we have no sin, we deceive ourselves, and the truth is not in us. If we confess our sins, he is faithful and just to forgive us our sins, and to cleanse us from all unrighteousness."

If someone says that they have not sinned, they are insensitive, so that person is not being true and has not been truly converted. As I have already said, it is the mark of the true Christian to be sensitive to sin itself. They are sensitive to evil. Because they have the new nature of God within them, such a person cannot condone the things of this world. They cannot go unscathed to a nightclub, they cannot condone drinking, drugs, and sensuality. They cannot walk in the midst of people who sneer and mock God without their hearts being saddened.

The one who is born of God cannot even condone nominal Christians, who deny with their attitudes what their baptisms or professions of faith have affirmed. Ephesians 4:30 says, "And grieve not the holy Spirit of God, whereby ye are sealed unto the day of redemption." This text shows that the Holy Spirit is saddened. What is he saddened with? Sin. The Holy Spirit dwells in every Christian, so they have in themselves the nature of God living in their hearts. When Christians sin, the Holy Spirit who dwells in them is saddened, and they too become saddened.

You know a true Christian by seeing their cry, their sensitivity to sin. This is evidence that the Holy Spirit of God, who is pure and does not tolerate sin, dwells in them and leads them to repentance.

Why does the true Christian cry? Because their crying is the result of them being poor in spirit! The moment they see the Law of God, with its righteousness, holiness, and perfection they immediately empty themselves and recognize their inability to be accepted by God. By emptying themselves from their own merits, they cry—cry for seeing their spiritual poverty.

A few years ago, a young man came into my office who at that time had been converted for two years. He had received many gifts and blessings in those days. Also, about that time, I had preached about someone "reaping what they had sowed." In the sermon I quoted some personal blessings that the Lord had given me after years of work and fidelity. The young man began to cry in front of me, saying, "Pastor, you have reaped many things that you planted justly. But I... I have never planted anything! Why am I reaping these things pastor?" At that very moment I was aware that before me was someone poor in spirit, who recognized that he did not deserve God's mercies.

On another occasion, talking to a newly-married man, I heard from him how weak he was, that he was not capable of facing the situations he was in. He was a truly burdened person, saddened by his own state. Again, I realized that he was a blessed man. There, before me was a man, who was poor, meek, and pure of heart. He was stripped of all arrogance and self-righteousness, with great conviction of his inability, just as the Lord had described that the poor in spirit would weep! So, he was happy, blessed, and complete!

In addition to weeping for sin itself, the true Christian cries for evil, for the sinfulness that exists in the world. It is the cry for sin at all levels of society: for rulers, prevailing laws, corrupt culture—for all areas of life that cause pain in God's creation and steal the glory He is due.

Something I have preached about regularly is the indifference of the people of God. Unfortunately, indifference has become the mark of the church in these last days. They are selfish, vain and narcissistic people, who are only concerned with themselves and their benefits, but cannot see the ills surrounding them. It seems like they see the news in the newspapers, magazines and social media, but they don't care about anything. They can read and watch moving atrocities by remaining impassive, without demonstrating any dismay or compassion! When speaking about the second beatitude, Jesus was teaching that blessed are those who care, who have pity on the misery of others, who feel acute pain for the sinfulness all around them. People who cannot hear blatant cases of pedophilia without feeling deep sadness; who feel the desperation of millions of starving people in the world while tons of food are wasted daily; they look at the escalation of the homosexual movement with grief because it stains the family that God established, yet at the same time they're willing to love and help the homosexuals, while openly and frankly condemning their conduct—these are the ones Jesus refers to as happy as they mourn.

How, reader, do you become desensitized with so much pain, sin, and frustration in your own family? In the people you work with? How many cases of adultery do you hear of people who are close to you? Do you feel the pain of the abandoned, the frustrated children, the men and women who are torn apart by lies and betrayal?

What about the millions of "legal" and illegal abortions performed annually? Defenseless "fetuses" aborted in the mothers' wombs. Have you never seen them struggling, fighting for life, when they are unscrupulously persecuted by shock or suction devices, which steal from them the possibility of seeing the sun and the stars? Millions of children are cruelly killed in cold blood, thrown into trash cans, gutters and toilets around the world that they have never had the opportunity to see and explore.

Would it be possible to maintain indifference when we are massacred with so many cases of persecution of our Christian brothers and sisters around the world, especially those being martyred, burned, beheaded, and abused by Muslims? How can one feel no pain for the Christian families who are meaninglessly and brutally killed by these criminals?

Would these cases not be enough for the tears to flow spontaneously from the eyes of God's people, mourning the destruction caused by sin around the globe?

How can we forget the systematic degradation of the entire biosphere of the Earth? How many millions of miles of forest are criminally destroyed or burned annually? How many river springs and their water basins, together with the seas, are polluted by heavy metals from mining, by the disorderly extraction of oil and by the dumping of sewage without treatment? Air quality worsens year after year with the emission of toxic gases into our atmosphere, all in favor of keeping the human consumption machine running. Animals are cruelly taken from their natural habitats—failing to maintain their stable communities, when they are not uncontrollably killed—in breeding periods.

Romans 8:20–23 says, "For the creature was made subject to vanity, not willingly, but by reason of him who hath subjected the same in hope,

Because the creature itself also shall be delivered from the bondage of corruption into the glorious liberty of the children of God. For we know that the whole creation groaneth and travaileth in pain together until now. And not only they, but ourselves also, which have the first fruits of the Spirit, even we ourselves groan within ourselves, waiting for the adoption, to wit, the redemption of our body."

Paul is arguing that sin has thrown the beautiful creation of God into collapse, causing it to suffer birth pains until the total redemption of the world is finally finished with Christ's return. Each micro-organism, plant, fish, reptile, bird, and mammal await their release from the bondage of corruption and degradation to which they were subjected by the Fall of Adam and Eve.

The apostle also argues that even the children of God also weep, groaning in their hearts in expectation of that blessed day when this scoured and decayed body will be clothed with incorruptibility and immortality, with the reward of being like the glorious body of our Lord Jesus Christ!

I want to tell you one thing: if you are indifferent to these things, if the degradation of the world and of humanity does not cause you sorrow, you must review your conversion. There is a great probability that you will not be saved if you live day after day without feeling even sorrow for your sins and for the pain of the world that is around you.

How can we not cry when watching numerous videos of pastors who blaspheme Christ's cross openly? Men who are reprobate, dirty, and scoundrels, who do everything for the undivided desire for power, pleasure, and personal fulfillment. People who commit scandalous sins—even in the eyes of the world—in the name of Christ! Such people are not pastors, but wolves eager to steal all that their sheep possess, and then to dispose of them mercilessly.

They are false prophets, who profit from Christ's cause, denying the truth of the Scriptures, leading thousands through tortuous paths that will never give them freedom and salvation. Because of these mercenaries, the "name of God is blasphemed among the Gentiles" (Rom 2:24). The true church, the people of God, cry out for the sins of false Christians, who scandalize the faith and afflict the people who follow Christ.

Biblical Examples of Those Who Mourn

See Jesus Christ, the Messiah of Israel, moved by the sin of his people in Matthew 23:37: "O Jerusalem, Jerusalem, thou that killest the prophets, and stonest them which are sent unto thee, how often would I have gathered thy children together, even as a hen gathereth her chickens under her wings, and ye would not!"

Note that the Bible teaches that the great goal for every Christian's life is to be similar to Christ, as Paul said in Romans 8:29: "For whom he did foreknow, he also did predestinate to be conformed to the image of his Son, that he might be the firstborn among many brethren." Our trajectory on earth consists of being molded in the likeness of Jesus, making us more and more like him.

The apostle John in 1 John 2:6 said, "He that saith he abideth in him ought himself also so to walk, even as he walked." Therefore, our goal is to walk like Jesus, to bear and to conduct our lives as he did. Our standard for imitation is Jesus Christ.

It is interesting that the Scriptures do not record Jesus making jokes and parodies. I do not mean that Jesus was not cheerful and complete. He rejoiced greatly, on various occasions, but we have a large number of passages reporting Jesus's agony, sorrow, and pain for the world's sinfulness. Jesus was not, in any way, like many current pastors who joke around in the pulpit, entertaining people with jokes and saying things with a double meaning. No, the Word of God was solemn. He knew very well what his mission was and the pain that it involved: to be the ransom of fallen humanity and the model for the redeemed humanity.

Pastors who make a mockery of God and fool around in his name, who think that the church of Christ should be entertained with "stand-up comedy gospel" will give an account before God, as Paul predicted in Galatians 6:7, "Be not deceived; God is not mocked: for whatsoever a man soweth, that shall he also reap." There will be a day that the Lord will ask each of these leaders to account for their words and actions in the face of his holiness.

What is the blessed reward promised by the Lord Jesus to the blessed who mourn for sin? Those who mourn for their sin were convinced by their God; those who have been convinced of sin have been regenerated; those who have been regenerated will repent from their sin; those who repent from sin and have faith in Christ will be saved! This is God's great consolation for those who weep for their sin.

Isaiah 1:18 brings a great promise to these happy citizens of heaven, "Come now, and let us reason together, saith the LORD: though your sins be as scarlet, they shall be as white as snow; though they be red like crimson, they shall be as wool." Have you been made white as snow, white as wool? Have your iniquities been washed away? Oh, what joy! The condemnation of God no longer hangs over your life. Psalm 130:7 confirms, "Let Israel hope in the LORD: for with the LORD there is mercy, and with him is plenteous redemption." You received consolation; you were redeemed!

God's forgiveness reaches all who weep, see Psalm 130:3–4, "If thou, LORD, shouldest mark iniquities, O Lord, who shall stand? But there is forgiveness with thee, that thou mayest be feared." Together with forgiveness, peace is received, God's consolation is enjoyed, relief of burdens and oppression arrives, and rest is finally received, as Jesus said in

Matthew 11:28–30, "Come unto me, all ye that labour and are heavy laden, and I will give you rest. Take my yoke upon you, and learn of me; for I am meek and lowly in heart: and ye shall find rest unto your souls. For my yoke is easy, and my burden is light."

For those who weep, a new chance to start again is given, just as Christ forgave the adulterous woman and allowed her to be, in peace, enjoying a new beginning, a new life free from sin and condemnation (John 8:1–11).

Conclusion

You may have read until here, but still say, "I am a Christian. I know of God's forgiveness and goodness for me and I weep, but I am still saddened and I have no complete consolation."

Calm down, dear brother in Christ, the full consolation of God will not be enjoyed on this side of heaven. It is reserved for eternity, as Romans 8:18 teaches, "For I reckon that the sufferings of this present time are not worthy to be compared with the glory which shall be revealed in us" and Revelation 21:3–4 says, "And I heard a great voice out of heaven saying, behold, the tabernacle of God is with men, and he will dwell with them, and they shall be his people, and God himself shall be with them, and be their God. And God shall wipe away all tears from their eyes; and there shall be no more death, neither sorrow, nor crying, neither shall there be any more pain: for the former things are passed away."

In heaven, the glory of God will supply everything we have lacked in this world. Any loss borne here will be fully rewarded. There, those who have wept here will have their tears washed away, their mourning will be turned into joy, and throughout eternity, they will enjoy the divine consolation.

CHAPTER 5

Blessed Are the Meek

After our Lord spoke about the poor in spirit and those who mourn, he began to deal with one of the most cherished qualities of mankind: meekness. In this chapter we will examine Matthew 5:5, "Blessed are the meek: for they shall inherit the earth."

Once again, when dealing with meekness, it is important to note that the Beatitudes are not natural traits; they are not qualities that a person can develop apart from God's grace and the help of his Spirit. Perhaps when talking about the quality of someone being meek, an unbeliever may come to mind whom you think of as exhibiting meekness. I want to stress that this is not the true meekness that Jesus is talking about here.

Only someone who has been regenerated by the Holy Spirit can be meek. The Beatitudes are the fruit of a transformed life, which only the saved hold possess. They are qualities that distinguish God's people from those who are not, for they are the authenticating marks—made by the Savior—in their unique character. The evidence that only Christians can be meek becomes more evident when the values of a Christian are in contrast to the current values of human society. Why is this?

We must recall from the first chapter the original audience of the Sermon on the Mount; there were many people who belonged to Jewish groups who expected the liberation of the Jews from Roman oppression by the Messiah. The heavy taxes, the lack of freedom, the domination by a foreign and pagan people were situations that needed to be resolved firmly and with fighting.

For the secular standards of that time—and of today too—the meek never stood a chance of gaining any advantage or raising profits, without a fierce fight. Imagine the controversy when Jesus said that, even in the hardships caused by Roman domination, men should be meek! However revolting this seemed, that was exactly his statement: the subjects of the kingdom of God would have to be meek, the law of the new covenant would require every believer to be meek, and that as children of God, they should not seek revolutionary means for the constitution of their inheritance.

When Jesus spoke of meekness, did he only mean to abstain from resisting against something unfavorable? Or perhaps he meant the absolute pacifist stance, which condemns any kind of just reaction against an unfair offender? We need to know, before we move forward, what being meek does not mean in the context of Scripture.

False Perceptions of the Meek

The quality of being meek is not a natural attribute or quality transmitted genetically from one person to another. It is not something that can be inherited through bloodline, as if you could say, "I am meek because my mother was meek, and her mother before her." Similarly, being meek is not something that can be developed or trained; one does not learn this characteristic at school or in an etiquette training course. It is not only the educated who can achieve a higher standard of meekness.

Many think that a person who is polite and placid exudes meekness. We are not talking about the differences between those who are frivolous or introspective, or introverted or extroverted; this is not about habits or temperaments. Furthermore, meekness is not diplomacy, good manners, or a refined education.

A common misconception of meekness refers to one being shy. There are those who think that a meek person is retracted, crestfallen, the quiet one in the classroom, or the quiet and obedient child in the home. Likewise, meekness does not mean a person is a coward, indolent, or omissive.

Jesus was meek, as Matthew 11:29 says, "Learn of me; for I am meek and lowly in heart"; however we can see him acting forcefully against those who were using the Temple of God inappropriately, in John 2:13–16:

> And the Jews' passover was at hand, and Jesus went up to Jerusalem. And found in the temple those that sold oxen and sheep and doves, and the changers of money sitting: And when he had made a scourge of small cords, he drove them all out of the temple, and the sheep, and the oxen; and poured out the changers' money, and overthrew the tables; And said unto them that sold doves, Take these things hence; make not my Father's house an house of merchandise.

Jesus did not hesitate in using force to expel from the Temple those who used that holy place to profit from their sales. He was firm and he used authority, so meekness cannot be confused with passivity, timidity, or cowardice.

Moses, the friend of God, received the title of the meekest man on earth (Num 12:3). After forty days at the top of Mount Sinai, he went down to find a people who had built the golden calf and were involved in drunken orgies. Without wavering, Moses summoned the faithful from the midst of Israel, ordering them to kill by the sword those who had fallen into sin (Exod 32:25–29), resulting in the death of three thousand people. Moses was meek, but he was not omissive in acting severely when the situation demanded it. These examples show us that being meek is not a quality of temperament, nor can it be confused with timidity and cowardice.

Being meek furthermore does not mean being complicit with everything and everyone, trying to keep the peace at any cost. There are those who try to keep the peace regardless of right and wrong, who "look the other way," trying to do everything in order not to take a stand.

It is those who do not have an opinion—or do not express it for convenience—who are happy with either the right or the wrong, as long as it does not create animosities. They are waverers, and this attitude is completely wrong; it is strongly condemned in the Sermon on the Mount by Jesus, "But let your communication be, yea, yea; nay, nay: for whatsoever is more than these cometh of evil" (Matt 5:37). We are called to take a stand, not try to find the path of least resistance.

After biblically examining what it means to not be meek, let us now understand what Jesus had in mind when he said that they were happy, complete, and meek.

True Nature of the Meek

Charles Spurgeon said that "being meek is not a virtue, it is grace." So, meekness is a divine gift, given to the Christian by the Holy Spirit. Galatians 5:22–23 says, "But the fruit of the Spirit is love, joy, peace, longsuffering, gentleness, goodness, faith, meekness, temperance: Against these things there is no law." The meekness to which Jesus refers in the Beatitudes is the same stated in the fruits of the Spirit reported in

Galatians. The meek person has received grace or God's favor to be able to exemplify that spiritual characteristic.

The Greek term used by Jesus for meek is praus, which means humble, moderate, and mild. The use of this word referred to the idea of an animal, a wild beast that was dominated, contained, and controlled. How can this be applied to the character of the true Christian? The Christian's compulsive, malignant and animalistic nature was dominated after conversion. He is no longer a slave to sin, but possesses the righteousness of Christ as a child of God (Rom 6:14, 8:21).

The old man is being mortified by the Holy Spirit (Rom 8:13, Col 3:5), so as the new man, the Christian has his faculties, desires, and compulsions controlled. For this reason he can be meek, for the Spirit of God is continually at work in him, giving him the fruit of the new life in Christ.

The person who was born again—and only that person—is able to control their desires: "He that is slow to anger is better than the mighty; and he that ruleth his spirit than he that taketh a city" (Prov 16:32). In this way, being meek is not being weak, indifferent, shy, or cowardly. The meek have strength, talent, and disposition dominated by the Holy Spirit. They rule and control themselves. The Puritan Thomas Watson (1620–1686) defined meekness as, "A grace through which we are empowered by the Spirit of God to control our passions."

Biblical Examples of the Meek

Now I will point out features that allow us to biblically discern the meek character of the true Christian. The first characteristic is that they exercise control over their will. The meek do not anger easily, are not sensuous, are not foul-mouthed, do not spend compulsively, are not stingy, do not boast, nor do they live opulently. It is someone whose spiritual nature controls their natural behaviors.

You will see that a meek person's standard of life is balanced, hardly committing excesses in their conduct. This does not mean that they are not tempted, do not commit sins, and do not deal with desires and problems. But it means that they, through the grace of God, exercise self-control, always leaning toward what is pleasing to God, as Paul said in Romans 8:5–6, "For they that are after the flesh do mind the things of the flesh; but they that are after the Spirit the things of the Spirit. For to be carnally minded is death; but to be spiritually minded is life and peace."

The second characteristic is that they are submissive to the will of God. There is a principle placed in the heart of the meek that will never allow them to rebel against God and his will revealed to him by Scripture. In any area of life that the meek discover God's will, they will bow down, however tempting it might be to disobey.

Even if they do not understand, even in times of harsh trial, in situations even involving tragedies, rebellion will not be a valid option to which they would follow. The meek believe their faith cannot be abandoned, their God must not be questioned, and surely the guilt for suffering is not of the Lord; divinity cannot be blasphemed, for his orders are not open to dispute. Even when man might stand alone (remember Moses as he descended from Mount Sinai), he remains firm and unshakable.

Remember Job? In one day, he received the news that all his oxen, sheep, asses, and horses were decimated, together with all his workers. While recovering from the information that he had become—from one hour to the next—poor and unstaffed, someone gave him the news, "All your sons and daughters were killed in a devastating disaster" (Job 1:13–19).

What was the reaction of the meek Job? See Job 1:20–22, "Then Job arose, and rent his mantle, and shaved his head, and fell down upon the ground, and worshipped; and said, naked came I out of my mother's womb, and naked shall I return thither: the LORD gave, and the LORD hath taken away; blessed be the name of the LORD! In all this Job sinned not, nor charged God foolishly." He did not condemn God, he did not sin against the Lord, he did not complain about his condition. We do not see a word of complaint against God in the mouth of that righteous man.

Shortly after this episode, to intensify Job's misery, his health was struck by a terrible disease, which punished him from head to toe (Job 2:7–8). There was that man—whom God had called upright (Job 1:8)—in the deepest misery and agony. He felt pain, lamented his condition, but at no time did he attribute any lack to God: "What? shall we receive good at the hand of God, and shall we not receive evil? In all this did not Job sin with his lips" (Job 2:10b).

Dear reader, how many people within the church cannot bear any loss or deprivation? They complain about life, wages, their spouse, pain and illness, about the worship, Christian service, the pastor, the preaching, and the church. Everything for them is difficult, upsetting, and problematic, because they always live in anxiety and bitterness, irate and complaining against God. That is absolutely not the conduct of someone who is saved.

I would like to remind you that God tests his people, as you can see in Deuteronomy 8:2–5:

> And thou shalt remember all the way which the LORD thy God led thee these forty years in the wilderness, to humble thee, and to prove thee, to know what was in thine heart, whether thou wouldest keep his commandments, or not. And he humbled thee, and suffered thee to hunger, and fed thee with manna, which thou knewest not, neither

did thy fathers know; that he might make thee know that man doth not live by bread only, but by every word that proceedeth out of the mouth of the LORD doth man live. Thy raiment waxed not old upon thee, neither did thy foot swell, these forty years. Thou shalt also consider in thine heart, that, as a man chasteneth his son, so the LORD thy God chasteneth thee.

What is the reason for God to have treated the Israelites with many trials in the wilderness? It was to test them, in an irrefutable way in their thoughts, words, and actions to see whether they were meek or not, whether they were submissive to God or not.

Psalm 37:4 says, "Delight thyself also in the Lord: and he shall give thee the desires of thine heart." What does "delight thyself" mean? It means to submit to what God is proposing in your life—be it good or evil. Thus we know the meek: they do not contend with God or separate from him in rebellion. The true Christian thinks, "Who art thou that repliest against God? Shall the thing formed say to him that formed it, why hast thou made me thus?" (Rom 9:20).

The Apostle Paul taught the "master class" about obedience to God's will in Philippians 4:11–13: "Not that I speak in respect of want: for I have learned, in whatsoever state I am, therewith to be content. I know both how to be abased, and I know how to abound: everywhere and in all things I am instructed both to be full and to be hungry, both to abound and to suffer need. I can do all things through Christ which strengtheneth me."

Imprisoned in Rome, suffering various deprivations, Paul said he was happy with what he had. If that was God's will for him, it didn't matter what he was going through, he relied on the Lord's sovereign decision concerning his state. Who was he to choose his lifestyle? In analyzing the complete passage, we see that Paul suffered a great many deprivations, yet he could endure because he was marked by blessed meekness.

A third characteristic we can see is that he readily obeys God's Word. The meek not only passively submit their lives to God's will, but they also joyfully obey the commands contained in the Word of God, as it is written in James 1:21 (NIV), "Therefore, get rid of all moral filth and the evil that is so prevalent and humbly accept the word planted in you, which can save you."

This text teaches that the meek welcome and receive with care the Word of God into their heart. They are subject to the Lord's commandments, sincerely wanting to obey them. The meek do not create their own rules, they do not follow the path they want, nor do they establish their own personal law. The meek obey God and only him as the one and only Lord. They strive to walk down the narrow path that keeps them in intimate fellowship with their Master.

What an example meek David was! Although sinful and a transgressor, when he was surprised by the prophet Nathan's rebuke of his sin with Bathsheba, David laid down his weapons, did not argue, and simply acknowledged that he was guilty (2 Sam 12).

The rarely discussed centurion Cornelius adequately portrayed the character of the true son of God. After receiving the visitation of an angel, he promptly sent people to call the Apostle Peter, as he had been instructed. Upon Peter's arrival, Cornelius declared, "Immediately therefore I sent to thee; and thou hast well done that thou art come. Now therefore are we all here present before God, to hear all things that are commanded thee of God" (Acts 10:33).

It was as if he had said, "I am ready, along with all my family, to hear all that God wants to speak through you." What were Peter's words? The inspired words of the New Testament, the canonic words of Scripture! Cornelius was saying that he would immediately obey the Word of God, which was proclaimed to him by the Apostle Peter. Peter preached to him the gospel of Christ, revealing that God was willing to save people from "any nation" (Acts 10:35). After he spoke, Peter was surprised, as he did not think that the Holy Spirit was for the Gentiles, for that "lower class" of people. This could have sounded like an affront to the ears of the centurion. However, meek Cornelius humbly heard Peter's exposition, and welcomed it with all joy in his heart.

Brother Andrew (founder of Open Doors Mission, author of God's Smuggler, responsible for taking illegal Bibles to the Soviet Union under a communist regime) tells an important personal testimony in one of his books. He received a letter from a certain woman, who accused him of many sins, discrediting and mocking him. When Andrew read the letter, he got angry and thought, "I'm going to write back and put this woman in her place." As he took the pen to write, the Spirit of God weighed on his heart, reminding him that, "blessed are the meek."

At the same time his mood changed and he wrote, "My dear, you are right. I am a sinner, and I have not only failed in these things, but if you had judged as God judges me and knew my sins as God knows, you would have written many more things. You could have increased even further my list of sins. My dear sister, you are right, I am a miserable sinner."

It is important for us to bear in mind how those who are not meek—in rebellion against the Word of the Lord—act. Their picture is painted in 1 Kings 22:7–9,

> And Jehoshaphat said, is there not here a prophet of the LORD besides, that we might enquire of him? And the king of Israel said unto Jehoshaphat, there is yet one man, Micaiah the son of Imlah, by whom we may enquire of the LORD: but I hate him; for he doth not prophesy good concerning me, but evil. This is Micaiah, son of Imlah. And Jehoshaphat said, Let not the king say so. Then the king

of Israel called an officer, and said, Hasten hither Micaiah the son of Imlah.

Ahab eventually recognized that there was a prophet of God, through whom his holy Word could be heard, but the wicked king despised this prophet, because his words always confronted his sin and wickedness. Ahab did not follow the commandments of God, and he hated Micaiah the prophet. The wicked king of Israel deeply disliked the word of the Lord, extending his hatred toward all those who were his messengers.

Another trait of the meek is that they graciously bear slander about them. The meek withstand lies, insults, bad treatment, and persecution without retaliation. It is plausible to say that all people at some point in their lives have been criticized and subjected to some sort of outrage, or have heard someone unjustly "give them a piece of their mind." How can we distinguish meekness in the receiver in these situations? They will not answer back to an affront. They will not get angry and lose self-control easily. They will not respond aggressively or seek to attack the offender in retaliation.

The Bible teaches that we must imitate the Lord Jesus. How did our Master act while being slandered and accused unjustly in the moments that preceded the crucifixion? Let's look at Luke 22:63–65,

And the men that held Jesus mocked him,

> and smote him. And when they had blindfolded him, they struck him on the face, and asked him, saying, prophesy, who is it that smote thee? And many other things blasphemously spake they against him.

They covered the eyes of the Savior, so that Jesus did not see who was hitting him. Worse, by covering his eyes, he would not know from whence the blows came, causing greater suffering under this aggression. However, to make it worse, they mocked the Lord asking him to prophesy who had wounded him. Our God was tortured and humiliated, beaten like a cornered animal. He—who with only the word of his mouth could destroy all those wicked men and condemn them succinctly—could have exercised all his power and stop the aggression.

Yet Jesus did not seek his rights, did not react abruptly or try to pay back the offense; he bore everything silently and did not open his mouth (Isa 53:7). Jesus considered all those unjust offenses as an opportunity to glorify God by not striking back. He preferred to leave all justice in God's omnipotent hands, just as Romans 12:19 tells us, "Dearly beloved, avenge not yourselves, but rather give place unto wrath: for it is written, Vengeance is mine; I will repay, saith the Lord."

The meek, rather than getting revenge and exer'becausesing their own righteousness, confidently expect God to justify them. They pray for those who persecute them (Matt 5:44); they walk two miles for the one who forces them to walk one (Matt 5:41); they bless and do not curse (Luke 6:28); and they even rescue an enemy in a time of need (Prov 25:21).

The meek act this way becausee this attitude will bring judgment not on them, but on the ones who offend them. Their offenders will have "coals of fire upon their heads," giving room to the righteousness of God (Prov 25:22). A genuine Christian, regardless of the level of the offense, will not pay evil with evil (Rom 12:21).

Once again, we can see the meekness of Job, even as he suffered the loss of his property, children, and health and had to deal with his affronting wife. She, mocking his situation, cruelly told him, "Dost thou still retain thine integrity? Curse God, and die" (Job 2:9). What a test for the miserable Job! His wife, who should serve him as a consoling and reputable companion, was the instrument of his torture. Without the grace of God, Job would certainly have lost his temper, offending his wife violently or, worse, he would have accepted her terrible advice, abandoning his faith in God.

Job's response proves his meekness by rebuking his wife for her sin, while he justly defended God, showing that he had a plan for what he did, for better or worse: "Thou speakest as one of the foolish women speaketh. What? Shall we receive good at the hand of God, and shall we not receive evil? In all this did not Job sin with his lips" (Job 2:10).

Dear reader, we are in critical need of meek people, who do not abandon their faith in God even in the face of the harshest trials of life. Today we need robust and strong men and women of God who are willing to wait on him for their deliverance (Job 13:15), not taking revenge into their own hands, but trusting the judge of all the earth (Gen 18:25).

A fifth feature of the meek is they do not defend their own reputation. Most Christian churchgoers often have no difficulty in saying that they are "miserable sinners, weak, and in lack of divine help." However, if any ecclesiastical authority rebukes him as a sinner or if any brother points out any sin, very quickly we see a different side of the story. The person is resentful, does not tolerate correction, and is quite likely to say that the other person is "judging them."

Is that the attitude of a meek person? Not at all. When reprimanded, the meek agree with the reprover: "It's true, you're right!" They have no reputation, name, or pride of their own to defend. The truly meek person is totally submitted to the shame of the rebuke, knowing very well that their great Defender is at the right hand of God in heaven (Rom 8:33–34).

Then we see the sixth feature: their satisfaction with what God has given them. In Psalm 37, we find the end that is in store for those who live this beatitude: "Fret not thyself because of evildoers, neither be thou envious against the workers of iniquity. For they shall soon be cut down like the grass, and wither as the green herb. Trust in the LORD, and do good" (Ps 37:1–3).

This passage shows that the meek must not burn in anger or envy the powerful and wealthy people of this world (see Ps 37:7–9). The meek do not care about opulence, and nor are they desperate to amass mounds of earthly goods and prestige in this world that is passing away. They are not avid and greedy for material achievements, breaking God's principles, abandoning the faith, offending and undermining their fellowship with God and with people!

There are many who say they are Christians who are anxious about the dollar exchange rate, about the volatility of the stock exchange, about the "unmissable sales" and for all else that Western consumerism has engraved on their minds and hearts! Someone who is really meek, the true Christian, will not flaunt possessions or will not have their heart heavily burdened from the cares of this life, "Lay not up for yourselves treasures upon earth, where moth and rust doth corrupt, and where thieves break through and steal: but lay up for yourselves treasures in heaven, where neither moth nor rust doth corrupt, and where thieves do not break through nor steal: for, where your treasure is, there will your heart be also" (Matt 6:19–21).

What is the reward of those who are happy, complete and blessedly meek? They will not need to enter a wild competition for a place in the world. They will not be like the wicked, who fight, sell and buy, wasting time building fortunes that do not bring true joy.

Conclusion

The meek are joyful people who possess the earth, that is, they are content with what they have. They are not anxious and afflicted by something that they lack, for they lack nothing! If they have little they are content, if they have enough they are happy, and if they have much they use it for the glory of God and the advancement of his kingdom! The meek, the satisfied, are the ones who inherit the earth and able to enjoy it, not being like the wicked who will always be dissatisfied and incomplete.

Besides this aspect, the meek are those who, in fact, will inherit the true and final earth, the new heavens and the new earth, when God restores all things in the completeness of his kingdom! Blessed are the meek, for they will inherit eternity with Christ! They will have new life and a new home, forever, and that will never end. They will be fully satisfied and complete!

CHAPTER 6

Blessed are Those Who Desire Righteousness

The desire for justice is a characteristic that we not only see in our Lord Jesus, but it is also described as a trait of the true Christian in Matthew 5:6: "Blessed are they which do hunger and thirst after righteousness: for they shall be filled."

When a person feels pain, they will invariably seek help to make the pain cease. The pain of a cut, a migraine, pain in the bones or a toothache, acute pain in the abdomen, or even mental pain that is reflected in the physical pain will lead a person to seek means to be set free from the discomfort.

If this person sees a careless doctor, he will give them a pain killer to temporarily relieve their distress, but the problem that causes the pain will not be solved, causing the person to seek another doctor saying that they have not yet felt relief from the pain they are experiencing. If the new doctor is experienced and committed to his profession, he will carefully analyze the health of the person to discover the root of the problem, healing the cause (disease) so that the effect (pain) ceases.

The cause of human pain, in all its broad manifestations, is sin and spiritual death which is every man's inheritance (Eph 2:1). Any other way of dealing with human pain that does not primarily treat the state of condemnation will only sedate the pain, removing the problem momentarily, without properly curing the disease. For this reason, happiness and completeness can only be achieved with the gospel of Christ, which heals the root of the human problem, brings reconciliation with God (2 Cor 5:18–19), and gives true peace.

While knowing that only conversion fills the need of the human soul, in the Beatitudes we see Jesus teaching that one of the characteristics of the true Christian is to hunger and thirst for righteousness; that is, they should no longer seek the "pain killers" of the world and sin as the source for their satisfaction, but rather they should seek God's revealed will.

Speaking of "hunger and thirst," Jesus uses a figure of speech to represent desire, will, expectation, or yearning for something. Everyone has desires. There is not a single person on the face of the earth who does not want something. For those who do not know God, who live according to the course of this world, their lives are dominated by various idolatrous wills: power, money, fame, beauty, pleasure, recognition, revenge, achievements, and the list goes on. Thus the wicked are hungry, but they're hungry for the world and its attractions; they are hungry for the pride of life, and for the lust of their eyes and for the lust of the flesh (1 Jn 2:16).

The true Christian, when brought to Christ, goes through a process of profound transformation, which makes him a citizen of the kingdom of God—someone who is saved and blessed. It is also important to remember that conversion is not the same as being baptized in the waters, it is not participating in the Lord's Supper, it is not supposedly to "speak in strange tongues" nor to prophesy, it is not to have some ecclesiastical ministry or function, it is not even to be a martyr and to die for

Christianity. Conversion is the supernatural and all-powerful work of God's Holy Spirit in the heart of Adam's son, a corrupt sinner who loves sin and the desire of the flesh.

When a sinner is saved, he is transformed into a new creature, completely different from what he was before salvation. Anyone who one day expects to enter heaven must have passed through this great transformation, without which no one will see the Lord.

This beatitude, which talks about a person's hunger and thirst, provides a clear distinction of whether or not someone has been saved. How do you know if you, reader, have been saved? How do you make sure that this transformation has occurred in you? It is shown through the will and type of desire that governs your life. While the wicked have the desire that inclines toward the world and the pursuit of happiness by being satiated by sin, the true Christian is hungry, yearning for spiritual things; they dream of heavenly things.

If your will, dear reader, still remains as it was before you knew Christ, it is likely that the wonderful transformation of conversion has not yet occurred in your life. If that is the case, you still try to satisfy your hunger in what the world deems satisfying; your joy is still the joy of the wicked; your will is not aligned with God's but is rather bent for the world; body, beauty, goods, and money are still the main idols of your heart.

Not even miracles, blessings, healings, or answers to prayer can be the object of the hunger of a genuine Christian. A problem we have faced in our day is the proliferation of churches that embrace the so-called "prosperity gospel," promising their followers the fulfillment of the same desires they had in the world, but with a Christian demeanor and jargon! These leaders deceive their followers, making them believe that they can enjoy all the vanities of the world, and above all, do so with the blessing of God! It is a false gospel, teaching a false Christ, preached by false teachers, leading to false security, which will not save those who trust in them.

If someone has indeed been converted, God will not need to fulfill their ancient sinful desires, for what the person previously loved so much they now hate and look on with total disgust. Their heart has changed, their will can no longer be satisfied with the same delights, the world is no longer the target of their ambition; and so God has promised them a new heaven and a new Earth, where the righteousness that the believer so desires reigns (2 Pet 3:13).

A few years ago, I was preaching in Moscow, Russia. There I was received by medical students, who introduced me to a Brazilian student who was the top student in the college. He had passed with all averages above ninety-five percent, which gave him the very rare honor of receiving the Red Diploma—the greatest academic award that anyone could receive in Russia. He spoke several languages and was an expert in his medical area, even when he was still in college. With a title like that, he was preparing to study ophthalmology in the United States at Harvard. That young man had told me that his greatest desire was to be rich, to be able to live peacefully, and to buy a certain model Ferrari.

After a certain time, his Christian friends and a pastor of our church preached to him, and he became a Christian. I later met him in Brazil and asked him, "And your dreams of wealth, how are they going?" He replied to me, "Oh, I don't want that anymore, it was all rubbish." His will was changed by salvation!

There is an intentional sequence in the Beatitudes that we need to understand. Jesus did not organize them randomly, but with a well-defined purpose and order. When someone recognizes their poverty of spirit, they are led to weep for their state, which leads them to be meek, trusting that there is another (the Lord) who can do it completely. At this point, the person begins to desire the one whom they can trust completely—to be filled with God—and becomes hungry and thirsty for righteousness, anxious to receive what they want so much to be complete. In this way, the fourth beatitude finds its place in the Lord's ordered and logical sequence by design.

What indeed is this righteousness for which the true Christian hungers and thirsts? It simply means the desire to grow in the likeness of Jesus Christ, our great standard of righteousness. The truly converted man desires spiritual virtue and growth and is not conformed by the spiritual death from which they came. His aim is to develop even more fully in the new life he received from the Lord (Eph 4:13).

In this development, the Christian's desire is to always become more righteous, more like Christ, which means to continually turn from sin and its practice in an ongoing process called sanctification. Sanctification begins immediately after someone's salvation, developing until their last day of life on earth.

As the Christian advances in knowledge of the Scriptures, his knowledge of God and of his own sinfulness is growing. This recognition of sin only comes by the Holy Spirit who leads the Christian to desire to overcome them through the mortification of sin. They can no longer live with their mistakes. Therefore, hunger and thirst for righteouesnss does not mean they will sin no more or be absolutely perfect. Rather, it means wishing to overcome sin, to resist its impulses, and to continuously fight against its enticements, keeping constant vigilance against the old man.

For the sincere Christian, the covenant with God made at their conversion is the most precious thing they possess. Nothing can tarnish or interrupt this blessed covenant by which they were brought back to the gracious Savior of their soul. To keep their fellowship with the Lord unobstructed, the Christian fights against sin, so that he does not tarnish his life with God (Isa 59:1–2) and grieve his Holy Spirit (Eph 4:30).

Another evidence of someone who hungers and thirsts for righteousness is that he does not fight hard only against sin, but also against the desire to sin. This struggle goes beyond the faults visible to men; this fight is found in the depths of the heart, expelling from there the evil intentions, judgments, the hatred that still remains, the envy, lust, vanity, immorality, and all the other horrible inclinations that still want to dominate their will.

See Romans 7:19, "For the good that I would I do not: but the evil which I would not, that I do." In this passage, the Apostle Paul showed the inner struggle of the Christian, as if he had said, "I don't want to do evil. I don't want to be haughty. I don't want to judge my brothers and sisters. I don't want to covet women and men, and I don't want to lie. My desire is that I would never sin." Therefore, the blessed, even though they sin, do not do so by premeditation. They fall by the weakness of their nature and no longer by devising ways of meeting the former desires of their flesh.

Now that we have looked at the negative aspect of sanctification—that of rejecting sin, separating from what is evil, and putting it to death (the mortification of sin)—now we turn to the positive aspect of sanctification: vivification. To hunger and thirst for righteousness speaks of the desire to be holy and pure. This process of vivification is carried out by the power of the Holy Spirit which enables a Christian to live a life that is irreproachable and without blemish, growing before God (2 Pet 3:14). The Apostle Paul in 1 Timothy 5:22 recommends, "Keep thyself pure." It is God's desire, placed in the heart of every new convert, that they are not only separated from evil, but that they should become more virtuous. They should be kept pure and grow in this purity. Therefore, to be holy is not only to hate evil, but to love goodness!

How many of you have seen someone who was converted recently? Have you seen how they struggle to please God in every aspect of their life? How they have the desire to conform their existence to the principles of God's Word in every little detail? They want to keep their body from sensuality, take care of their tongue, protect their mind and thoughts, desire to keep and build their children in the knowledge of the Lord, and are zealous with their finances and with the contribution to the advancement of God's work. They wish to grow in their sanctification for the Lord.

When they fall into sin, they feel sorrow; when they cannot read the Bible with dedication or truly pray, they cry; when they do not control themselves and fail, they dislike themselves completely. Examples such as these show their hunger and thirst for being perfect (complete) in righteousness before God (Matt 5:48). Do not be deceived, salvation does not have a degree, but sanctification differs in glory and intensity from one saved person to another, according to their dedication to the Lord.

This growth in sanctification walks in harmony with the knowledge of the Word of God. Sanctification in practice is to know and apply every concept of the Bible in daily life. A person who is hungry and thirsty for righteousness seeks to understand in detail and actually practice what the Scriptures teach in all aspects of life. They rejoice in every commandment of the Lord, seeking to diligently obey his will.

The one who desires the righteousness of God desires to manifest in their character all the Beatitudes of the Sermon on the Mount. His will is to be poor in spirit, to cry for sin, to be meek, to be merciful, to be a peacemaker, and to be clean of heart. His great intention is to follow the will of the Lord very closely. He also wishes to exhibit what is written in Galatians 5:22–23, "But the fruit of the Spirit is love, joy, peace, longsuffering, gentleness, goodness, faith, meekness, temperance."

Those who hunger and thirst for righteousness aim to be longsuffering, gracious, and meek; they desire to have self-control, to maintain joy, peace, love, and faith, because the fruit of the Holy Spirit is nothing more than the likeness of Jesus.

In addition to the qualities of character, someone with a desire for righteousness longs for God and his presence, as 1 John 1:3b says: "our fellowship is with the Father, and with his Son Jesus Christ." The desire of the Christian is to be close to God, to spend time with him, to know him more and more through prayer, the Bible, and meditation on his promises and warnings.

What has happened to our generation? Churchgoers enjoy the whole church service, except that which refers to the spiritual life! They despise public worship and preaching, secret prayer, growth in biblical knowledge, and private fasts; furthermore, many of today's church members do not have any interest in enjoyingthe presence of God.

It is the mark of someone who hungers and thirsts for righteousness, who wants to know more about God and desires more of his holy presence, that leads them to cry out: "O God, thou art my God; early will I seek thee: my soul thirsteth for thee, my flesh longeth for thee in a dry and thirsty land, where no water is" (Ps 63:1); "Seek the LORD, and his strength: seek his face evermore" (Ps 105:4); "And ye shall seek me, and find me, when ye shall search for me with all your heart" (Jer 29:13).

They who desire righteousness seek the Lord with all their heart, and seek his face continually; like the dry earth that needs rain, they seek God's presence. Their interest is not in miracles or temporary blessings; they want God—they desperately need God!

Using the terms hunger and thirst, the Lord makes the comparison to the two vital needs of every human being: eating and drinking. Without these resources, human life ends. The hunger that Jesus describes, however, is not the craving for a certain food or delicacy, nor does it mean missing breakfast and being anxious about lunch. The hunger described in the text is one of someone who has not eaten for ten, twenty, or thirty days. It is the famishment of the hungry, as the Jews experienced in the concentration camps of Nazi Germany in World War II. Those unjustly imprisoned died of starvation because they were hungry!

Likewise, the thirst described by Jesus refers to the person who is almost dying for lack of water. It is someone who painfully remains alive despite the extreme lack of water in their body. The image is of someone with cracked lips, blurred vision, and slow thoughts due to the absence of water.

It is this kind of need that Jesus taught would be supplied to the blessed who have it. It is this type of famishment and thirst that the Lord has placed within everyone who desires righteousness, fellowship with God, and his blessed Word.

When a person has this kind of need for God, they lose sleep and get up in the early hours of the day to pray privately with the Creator; they make use of every free time to read and meditate on the Scriptures; they take the opportunity to evangelize at all times, and when they cannot, they create an opportunity; they arrive earlier to church and leave later, wanting to spend most of their time in the fellowship of the saints; when you tell them about Elijah, John the Baptist, John Wesley, or George Whitefield they answer saying they want to be like them.

Scripture describes this state, "as newborn babes, desire the sincere milk of the word" (1 Pet 2:2). The Christian desires with a passion similar to that of babies for breast milk the doctrine of God and his presence.

"Therefore take no thought, saying, what shall we eat? What shall we drink? Or, Wherewithal shall we be clothed? (For after all these things do the Gentiles seek:) for your heavenly Father knoweth that ye have need of all these things. But seek ye first the kingdom of God, and his righteousness; and all these things shall be added unto you" (Matt 6:31–33). The Christian voluntarily puts aside essential natural needs to have the kingdom of God as a priority in life.

"After this manner therefore pray ye: Our Father which art in heaven, Hallowed be thy name. Thy kingdom come, Thy will be done in earth, as it is in heaven" (Matt 6:9–10). The great desire of this Christian is that the kingdom of God would be established, his will be fulfilled, and the whole Earth be covered with the glorious salvation of the Lord.

Jesus said, "Labor not for the meat which perisheth, but for that meat which endureth unto everlasting life" (John 6:27). Do not have as your goal to seek Christ only for the temporary and earthly blessings that he can give you. Seek him for the promises and spiritual food he offers. His great goal is not to satisfy your desires, but for you to glorify God and enjoy him forever.

True Nature of Those Seeking Righteousness

Let us look at some examples of people in the Bible who had a hunger and thirst for righteousness. First we see Zacchaeus, the publican (Luke 19:1–10). He was a rich tax collector who was at the service of Rome. He was a corrupt man, considered a traitor and thief by the other Jews. Zacchaeus's deepest desire was to be rich and prosperous. One day, as Jesus passed through Jericho, he decided to spend the night in Zacchaeus's house, and do you know what happened? He was converted; Zacchaeus was transformed! What was the attitude of that wicked tax collector on becoming a follower?

He gave the poor half of his fortune, and if he had defrauded someone, he would pay them four times the amount he had unjustly received! Zacchaeus ceased to be hungry and thirsty for money, and became hungry and thirsty for Jesus and for the righteousness of God! What was Jesus's response to this? "This day is salvation come to this house, forsomuch as he also is a son of Abraham. For the Son of man is come to seek and to save that which was lost" (Luke 19:9–10). The evidence that Zacchaeus entered the kingdom of heaven, was that he left his greed for profits to have an eagerness for the righteousness of God.

We can also see this example in Paul, the apostle to the Gentiles. See what this giant of the Christian faith said in Philippians 3:7–8, "But what things were gain to me, those I counted loss for Christ. Yea doubtless, and I count all things but loss for the excellency of the knowledge of Christ Jesus my Lord: for whom I have suffered the loss of all things, and do count them but dung, that I may win Christ."

He is simply stating that all which previously had some value to him—his Jewish descent, his high education, his honors—he considered as having no value for the privilege of being completely consumed in his desire to gain Christ. For Paul, everything outside of Christ was completely despicable, indeed, disgusting, for he compares it to rubbish (dung).

Thus the apostle saw his search for Christ—which involved hunger, danger, persecution, injustice, flogging, tiredness, a lot of pain and affliction, being misunderstood many times, and torture—as superior to any other glory or sacrifice that he would have to make to have the object of his obsession: the Lord Jesus Christ!

Because of Christ, Paul lost everything, including his life by being martyred by the government of Rome. He said he was willing to lose everything to "gain Christ." It was not to build a great ministry and receive recognition, it was not to have more power, it was not even to win souls or a heavenly reward! It was through the sublime privilege of knowing Christ, and having his hunger and thirst satisfied in God!

How can we not mention David, the man according to the heart of God (Acts 13:22)? Psalm 130:6 says, "My soul waiteth for the Lord more than they that watch for the morning." David spoke of the watchmen who looked out all night, protecting their positions as sentinels. In that state they felt cold, afraid, and lonely, eagerly waiting for the dawn to come, so that they could finish their shift and go to their homes to rest, to be with their wives, and to dwell in the warmth of their families. David used that language to say that he wanted God more than those guards wanted the dawn to come! He was hungry and thirsty for God!

Psalm 42:1–2 expresses once again David's longing for God's presence, "As the hart panteth after the water brooks, so panteth my soul after thee, O God. My soul thirsteth for God, for the living God: when shall I come and appear before God?"

Furthermore, Psalm 63:1 reports, "O God, thou art my God; early will I seek thee: my soul thirsteth for thee, my flesh longeth for thee in a dry and thirsty land, where no water is." In this psalm, David was fleeing from Saul, in the midst of a vast and terrible wilderness. As he hid, he probably saw people wandering through the wilderness, desperate and hungry for water, with their mouths cracked and weak voices. When writing the psalm, David said that his thirst for God was the same! He was about to die if he did not receive the blessed water from God's presence.

Note that he was not asking God for deliverance, nor was he asking for the death of his enemy Saul; he was not asking to be king or to receive blessings. He was praying that God would visit him in that inhospitable place; he was seeking to worship and be satiated by God in the midst of the desert! Blessed David, who longed for his God so much, soon he was heard and received his grace.

As a final example, I write with reverence of one of the greatest men to live: Moses. He saw his staff become a serpent, and he saw the terrifying plagues on Egypt, from frogs and lice to the death of the firstborn of all the families of Egypt. After the Red Sea opened in a stupendous miracle, he asked the Lord to close up the sea when the Egyptians tried to cross it, killing Pharaoh's army.

During the desert pilgrimage, he enjoyed a cloud covering the entire camp during the day and a column of supernatural fire warming them up during the night. The people were hungry, and Moses saw God feeding them with manna, the bread of heaven, in the midst of deep loneliness and aridity of the desert. As if it were not enough, God even brought quails to feed more than two million men in that inhospitable place!

In addition to experiencing the Lord's mercy and grace in all of this, he was the protagonist of some of the greatest miracles ever seen. He saw God write his Law on tablets of stones and was with him for forty days and forty nights. What else could such a man want? Exodus 33:18, replies, "And he said, I beseech thee, shew me thy glory."

After all of these tremendous events, Moses's great hunger and thirst was for God. He asked to see the face of Yahweh himself! It was as if he had said, "I don't need anything else, nothing else. I need the Lord God. I need your presence!" This is the great evidence of a genuine Christian: regardless of how much they may possess or enjoy the good gifts in this world, they will never be satisfied by them. Even though the Lord's blessings reach them, their hunger and thirst remains the same—to know God and to enjoy him!

It does not mean that an authentic Christian does not pray or seek God for their temporal needs. Absolutely not! Christians go to God for everything they need, but they do not go to the Lord only for the blessings or providence he can give. The Christian goes to God, despite all his needs, continually crying, "Lord, even though I have many needs, you are the one I need most. My desire is to have you, find you and be full of your presence—this desire is greater than all the other needs I can have."

Biblical Examples of Those Seeking Righteousness

What is the evidence that someone has hunger and thirst for righteousness?

One of the first ways to identify a Christian hungering and thirsting after righteousness is that they prioritize spiritual things and seek to be satisfied in them. Matthew 6:33 says, "seek ye first the kingdom of God, and his righteousness." Doing God's will in life is the priority of someone who desires righteousness. How is this priority expressed? Through their zeal for the Scriptures, their yearning for prayer, and their frequency in public services and spiritual fellowship with other brothers and sisters.

Another of the proofs that someone hungers and thirsts for God is that they are Bible scholars. See Joshua 1:8: "This book of the law shall not depart out of thy mouth; but thou shalt meditate therein day and night, that thou mayest observe to do according to all that is written therein: for then thou shalt make thy way prosperous, and then thou shalt have good success." The first instruction God gave Joshua, immediately after the death of Moses when Joshua had just taken over the leadership of Israel, was that his priority should be to meditate on, ponder, and deeply know the Word of God.

Psalm 1:1–2 repeats the same truth, "Blessed is the one who does not walk in step with the wicked or stand in the way that sinners take or sit in the company of mockers, but whose delight is in the law of the LORD, and who meditates on his law day and night." The mark of a blessed person is to be a scholar of Scripture. They consult the Scriptures in everything and go deep into the Word year after year, season after season; the more time passes, the more refined becomes their knowledge of the Word of God.

They do not do this as a burden or because they are obliged to, neither because they have to follow a religion. No, the blessed person finds their pleasure and delight in the Law of the Lord! They plan their whole day so that they can spend quality time with the Scriptures, delighting in its truths. When the needs of the day distract them, making it difficult to devote themselves to the study of the Word of God, they anxiously await the first opportunity to dive into the holy lines and find their joy there!

This was exactly the attitude of Ezra, in all his diligence toward the Scriptures, "For Ezra had prepared his heart to seek the Law of the LORD, and to do it, and to teach in Israel statutes and judgments" (Ezra 7:10).

Psalm 119 mightily sings of the joy of a blessed person with the Word of God: "O how I love thy law! It is my meditation all the day!" (v. 97); "I will meditate in thy precepts and have respect unto thy ways" (v. 15); "Thy word is very pure: therefore thy servant loveth it" (v. 140); "Thy word is a lamp unto my feet, and a light unto my path" (v. 105); "Order my steps in thy word: and let not any iniquite have dominion over me" (v. 133); "I rejoice at thy word, as one that findeth great spoil" (v. 162). What amazing texts! This psalm speaks of loving the Law of God, meditating on and respecting his commandments, cherishing it more than gold, following its guidance, enjoying and being satiated by it, and finding pleasure in the Word of God. Let me ask you, dear reader: do you consider the Word as your greatest spoil, your greatest treasure? The Puritans called the Scriptures the Holy Book, or the Book of God. They said it was physically like a mouth, where the Old Testament was one lip and the New Testament the other! Their love of God's Word was so much that the Puritan Thomas Cartwright (1535–1603) once said, "Lord, whatever you do with us, do not take away the Bible from us; kill our children, burn down our houses, destroy what we have, but spare us your Bible, don't take your Bible from us." Anyone who has hunger and spiritual thirst needs to go to the Word of God, so "that he might make thee know that man doth not live by bread only, but by every word that proceedeth out of the mouth of the LORD doth man live" (Deut 8:3, Matt 4:4).

Another non-negotiable priority of those who hunger and thirst for righteousness is prayer. What was the mark of the disciples closest to Jesus? Prayer: "But we will give ourselves continually to prayer, and to the ministry of the word" (Acts 6:4); "Now Peter and John went up together into the temple at the hour of prayer, being the ninth hour" (Acts 3:1). Prayer enabled them to do the tasks of ministry, gave them fellowship with God, consoled them, mortified their sin, filled them with the Holy Spirit, and overcame the powers of darkness. If prayer was vital to the first apostles, those who walked with Jesus, how much more is it vital for us?

Have you experienced the sweet blessing of prayer? When you begin to pray, you're hungry and tired, broken in sin and discouraged; then suddenly, you are nourished, sanctified, and comforted. You get up from prayer as a giant, completely remade!

Let us look to the Apostle Paul: "Therefore loosing from Troas, we came with a straight course to Samothracia, and the next day to Neapolis; and from thence to Philippi, which is the chief city of that part of Macedonia, and a colony: and we were in that city abiding certain days. And on the Sabbath we went out of the city by a river side, where prayer was wont to be made; and we sat down, and spake unto the women which resorted thither" (Acts 16:11–13). The apostle was traveling and had just arrived at Philippi, when immediately he sought a place where he could pray. It was as if he had said, "I have to speak to God. I have to fill myself with God, and have fellowship with him. I will only know how to act in every step I take in this place if the Lord leads me!"

Furthermore, Jesus, the second person of the Trinity, God-man, prayed deeply and at length, "And it came to pass in those days, that he went out into a mountain to pray, and continued all night in prayer to God" (Luke 6:12). Interestingly, prayer was never sporadic in Jesus's life, but it was something constant, "When Jesus had spoken these words, he went forth with his disciples over the brook Cedron, where was a garden, into the which he entered, and his disciples. And Judas also, which betrayed him, knew the place: for Jesus ofttimes resorted thither with his disciples" (Jn 18:1–2). Why did Judas know that place so well? Because Jesus often gathered together with his disciples to pray.

The proof that someone hungers and thirsts for God is that they cannot stay long away from prayer. Fellowship with God in prayer is their fuel, the flame of their soul, and their burning desire! They cannot conceive the idea of facing the day without invoking the name of the Lord, of dealing with the problems that arise without divine help, or of sleeping without having spoken to the Savior. They may have been busy or feel tired, but there is an inner principle that drives them to prayer. They live their lives waiting for an opportunity to be alone with God.

In contrast, if you talk to someone who does not hunger and thirst for righteousness, you will see the excuses this person will give when the subject of prayer is addressed. They will try to change the subject, being angry and armed with justifications and excuses so that they needn't pray. Why does this occur? Because this person's desire does not rest on having personal fellowship with God. They may even like to speak of God and his greatness, but they know very little of the person of God.

Having a desire for righteousness still involves being assiduous in the public service to the Lord. It is the great joy of the faithful to know that there is a public meeting with other worshipers that they can go to and praise the holy majesty of God. Psalm 122:1 states, "I was glad when they said unto me, let us go into the House of the LORD." David was saying that he was filled with joy by going to the house of God, worshiping him publicly with other brothers and sisters, participating in the fellowship, being taught by preaching, and being filled with the Spirit of God. For this reason he always went to the House of God: "Lord, I have loved the habitation of thy house, and the place where thine honor dwelleth" (Ps 26:8).

The New Testament records that it was common for the disciples of the Lord to gather in the temple, "And they worshipped him, and returned to Jerusalem with great joy: and were continually in the temple, praising and blessing God" (Luke 24:52-53); "And they, continuing daily with one accord in the temple, and breaking bread from house to house, did eat their meat with gladness and singleness of heart, praising God, and having favor with all the people. And the Lord added to the church daily such as should be saved" (Acts 2:46-47).

After that, the church began to gather in houses, always practicing worship, prayer, the reading of the Word, preaching, baptism, and the Lord's Supper. The public meeting was so important for Christian spiritual growth that the abandonment of this duty was considered a serious sin, "Not forsaking the assembling of ourselves together, as the manner of some is; but exhorting one another: and so much the more, as ye see the day approaching" (Heb 10:25). The desire for righteousness in a true Christian will always encourage him to honor and to participate in the fellowship of the visible church of the Lord on the earth.

Spiritual fellowship with other brothers and sisters is always appreciated by those who have a true hunger and thirst for righteousness. A Christian desires to have the company of another godly brother or sister to share with him or her the truths of the Bible. Having spiritual fellowship with other brothers and sisters helps to fill the heart of the Christian with the same grace and virtue that they received from God; it makes the Christian grow spiritually.

You will see that a Christian who is growing up in righteousness will always seek closeness with other believers who are more experienced than them in the way of the Lord. They want to hear his teachings, learn more from the Scriptures and from good theology, hear their personal testimonies and experiences with God, and they want their faith to be strengthened in the Lord!

This was the constant experience of the early church, narrated in Acts 2:42, "And they continued steadfastly in the apostles' doctrine and fellowship." Andrew was with John, who were together with Peter and James, who met with women to experience encouragement, exhortation, teaching, praying, and eating together!

Note that we are speaking here about spiritual fellowship, of friendship that builds up mutual faith. There is an important teaching about this in both the old and the new covenant, according to Proverbs 13:20, "He that walketh with wise men shall be wise: but a companion of fools shall be destroyed." Then in 1 John 1:7: "But if we walk in the light, as he is in the light, we have fellowship one with another."

The Christian bond of friendship always aims to communicate light, the life of God that we receive and share with other brothers and sisters. If friendship is not based on this principle—if fellowship does not have this purpose—then there will be no edification; but on the contrary, one person will hinder the other's spiritual growth.

A word of warning must be given: be careful of the meetings of "Christians" where the Word of God is not mentioned, where Christian purity and kindness is not exercised and, most importantly, where the main reason for the gathering is not for the glory of God and obedience to his commandments. See Paul advising his disciple Timothy on this subject, "Flee also youthful lusts: but follow righteousness, faith, charity, peace, with them that call on the Lord out of a pure heart. But foolish and unlearned questions avoid, knowing that they do gender strifes" (2 Tim 2:22–23). If the reasons for the "Christian" meetings are worldly, carnal, and trivial, then the apostolic council agrees in unison: escape!

According to evidence, the Christian seeking righteousness avoids all sin that prevents his spiritual progress. 1 Thessalonians 5:22, teaches, "Abstain from all appearance of evil." Another translation says, "Reject every kind of evil." The Christian who desires righteousness avoids, withdraws, and deviates from everything that prevents his spiritual progress. Paul taught the Thessalonians that they should move away and reject all appearance of evil, that is, any obstacle to their spiritual growth.

What should one leave in order to desire righteousness? Ungodly friendships, bad conversations, watching programs that do not edify, spending their time in a disordered and idle manner, going to places that are disagreeable to Christians. A true Christian will do whatever it takes to ensure that sin does not upset their fellowship with God.

Something that has greatly damaged the spiritual lives of many Christians today is the love of money. The church of our generation has been too comfortable with wealth, causing it to lose its calling and purpose in this world.

Ecclesiastes 5:10 says, "Whoever loves money never has enough; whoever loves wealth is never satisfied with their income. This too is meaningless." Solomon said that he who loves this will never be satisfied. Those who love wealth can never be complete. Why?

Let's look at the teaching of the New Testament, "but they that will be rich fall into temptation and a snare, and into many foolish and hurtful lusts, which drown men in destruction and perdition" (1 Tim 6:9). Those who love money and possessions will lose themselves completely, and end up ruining their lives. Do you know, dear reader, people who live day and night attracted to money, shopping, sales, profits, interest, and debt securities? Do you see that they are never satisfied? They never enjoy peace with the Lord?

Why, when "Christians" enter this illusion, can they not be satisfied? Because they invariably end up abandoning the faith, as 1 Timothy 6:10 says, "For the love of money is the root of all evil: which while some coveted after, they have erred from the faith, and pierced themselves through with many sorrows." By seeking to satisfy themselves in this world they ruin themselves, to the detriment of great pain and torment.

Those who desire to balance great accumulated riches with the Christian life will never be satisfied.

A third evidence of one who is seeking righteousness is that he avoids all licit things that could prevent spiritual growth. You see, this characteristic does not say that the blessed avoid sin only, but they avoid even what is not sin—that which is even lawful—but prevents them from deepening their hunger and thirst for God.

1 Corinthians 10:23 says, "All things are lawful for me, but all things are not expedient: all things are lawful for me, but all things edify not." Paul was teaching that all that God did not forbid in his Scripture is lawful, is allowed to the Christian. For example, playing sports, traveling and visiting places, studying hard for a public contest, or working a shift of ten or twelve hours—none of these things are forbidden to the Christian.

But the apostle placed an evaluation in his affirmation: "not everything is lawful, *not everything edifies*"; that is, it may not be sinful, but it could affect your fellowship with God. Do you restrict your growth in the righteousness of the Lord? Does what you've chosen to do prevent you from fulfilling other relevant spiritual functions? If the answer is yes, the genuine Christian will seek to remove from their way everything that hinders them from satisfying their hunger and thirst for God. With the spiritual sensitivity given to all Christians, each person who is full of the Spirit knows when they should not be in a certain place, should not have bought a certain thing, should not have compromised, or should not have been so busy with their well-being. It is not a question of legalism; but every sensitive Christian who has a close relationship with God always knows for what, where, and when to dedicate themselves.

So that they may remain on the narrow path that the Lord of glory gave them to walk along, the true Christian is disciplined in their life. They do not allow certain things, they are not self-indulgent with their desires, and they are moderate and have self-control in their choices and the things they are inclined towards. Once again I repeat, not because it is sin, but because it does not aid in satisfying the hunger and thirst that they have for God.

Another evidence we can see is that Christians intentionally discipline themselves to seek spiritual things. In this aspect we see the experienced Apostle Paul teaching his young disciple in 1 Timothy 4:7–8, "But refuse profane and old wives' fables, and exercise thyself rather unto godliness. For bodily exercise profiteth little: but godliness is profitable unto all things, having promise of that life that now is, and of that which is to come." The call was to be disciplined, to exercise in a way that achieves growth in piety through the spiritual exercises of prayer, study of Scriptures, and private fasting. You will always find discipline in someone who hungers and thirsts for God.

See Paul again talking about this issue: "But I keep under my body, and bring it into subjection: lest that by any means, when I have preached to others, I myself should be a castaway" (1 Cor 9:27). He was a busy apostle, who took care of many churches, feeling tiredness, loneliness—often under strong persecution; it was not uncommon for him to feel depressed and sad, and he went through many spiritual oppressions, material shortages, and was misunderstood even by Christians.

How was he disciplined? He taught that he submitted his body and desires to the service of the Lord. He fought against things that were not sin in themselves, so that he could serve his Savior more and better. He willingly made himself a slave of Christ and his gospel, and this was a great benefit of his spiritual life.

When we hunger and thirst for righteousness, we will always find time, resources, and conditions to satisfy our spiritual desire. The big question is: do we actually hunger for God? Are we willing to submit to military discipline (2 Tim 2:3–5) for the benefit of our spiritual growth and the goodness of the cause of Christ on earth? Are we slaves of the Master Jesus, to the extent that our licit desires are exchanged for his kind orders? Hunger and thirst for righteousness will always lead someone to fight fiercely to achieve the great purpose of their heart: being complete in Christ.

Dear reader, let me give you an example of what we have seen so far: if someone eats regularly, with four or five well-balanced meals per day, that person will have no shortage in their body. However, if they no longer have any meals, they may exhibit a slight change of mood, getting irritated. If they go a week without eating, there is a great likelihood of developing stomach problems and getting sick. If their food deprivation continues, that person is at serious risk of irreversible damage to their health, even at risk of death.

If you are not hungry and thirsty for righteousness, have no spiritual appetite, and do not go to God regularly to satisfy yourself, you can hardly be considered a Christian who is indwelled by the Holy Spirit! Think: if a person who eats regularly stops eating and loses their appetite, there is certainly something wrong with them. If nothing is done, then their health will wither. If this person continues in this state, they will need medical attention and a plan to regain their health.

Similarly, if a Christian does not demonstrate an appetite, hunger, and spiritual thirst for God, there is something wrong in their soul, which needs to be treated so that they do not wither completely. The loss of appetite for the Lord is an detrimental sign, showing that a serious illness is settling in the heart of the person which needs to be fought quickly.

There are people who say they are Christians, but do not pray at home, do not read their Bibles regularly, have no specific time for their daily time with the Lord, or never secretly fast to God. These people clearly show that they do not need God for their vital needs.

If the spiritual exercises and worship of the Lord—ordained by the Savior for the health and growth of everyone who is saved—are boring and tiring for you, if being a Christian is a burden to your existence, as if you were condemned to be holy, be careful! It is likely that there is no genuine salvation in your life. When was the last time you prayed in your room? When was the last time you read an entire book of the Bible? When was the last time you fasted, holy, zealous, and devoted exclusively to God? The terms used by Jesus for hunger and thirst indicate great need and desire for the things of God.

I ask you: do you think that the mere churchgoer can be a strong Christian—someone who only reads the Bible at the time of preaching, who only prays in a public service? Without regular feeding from God, how do you expect to be strong? How can you be holy and have a genuine interest for God's work in the world? How can you overcome Satan and his hosts? How can you triumph over the flesh and its more intense desires? Impossible!

Perhaps you ask yourself: does it mean that to be a Christian I have to do all of what has been described in this chapter to a level of perfection? No. We cannot always live at this spiritual peak. However, those who hunger and thirst for righteousness *desire* to have this standard of spiritual life. It's like the Puritan Christopher Love (1618–1651) who told his wife just before he was martyred in the Tower of London, "My most gracious beloved, you are interested in such a covenant that accepts purposes for performances, desires for deeds, sincerity for perfection, the righteousness of another—that of Jesus Christ—as it were your own alone. Oh! My love! Rest thou in the love of God, the bosom of Christ."

What promise does the beatitude of hunger and thirst for righteousness carry with it? What will the hungry and thirsty for God receive? What comes for those who yearn for the Savior and desire to be filled with his Holy Spirit?

Jesus said that they will be "satisfied." They will not live in search forever; there will be a period in which they will receive abundantly all they are seeking. This hunger and thirst will result in a full harvest of rightousness! John 6:35 says, "And Jesus said unto them, I am the bread of life: he that cometh to me shall never hunger; and he that believeth on me shall never thirst." Jesus taught that he himself would supply and satisfy all those who seek Him.

See these examples of God's promises of abundance the in his Word for those who desire righteousness:

Psalm 81:10: "I am the LORD thy God, which brought thee out of the land of Egypt: open thy mouth wide, and I will fill it." What a perfect analogy; Israel had just come out of the painful slavery in Egypt, in which they endured great hardship, hunger, and thirst. The Lord said to them, "Are you hungry, are you thirsty? Are you in need of something? Then open your mouths that I will fill them in abundance!"

Psalm 107:9: "For he satisfieth the longing soul, and filleth the hungry soul with goodness." The people of Israel were crossing the desert toward the land of Canaan. God did not let them perish from hunger or thirst. On the contrary, he filled the hungry soul with goodness, and he gave everything that was necessary for their journey; the good news is that he is still ready to give us today everything we need on our way to heaven!

Jeremiah 29:11–13: "For I know the thoughts that I think toward you, saith the LORD, thoughts of peace, and not of evil, to give you an expected end. Then shall ye call upon me, and ye shall go and pray unto me, and I will hearken unto you. And ye shall seek me, and find me, when ye shall search for me with all your heart." He promised, dear reader, that your search will not be in vain; you will find it.

Matthew 7:7–8: "Ask, and it shall be given you; seek, and ye shall find; knock, and it shall be opened unto you: For every one that asketh receiveth; and he that seeketh findeth; and to him that knocketh it shall be opened." Have you been seeking the Lord's presence? Then continue, because you *will* find Him.

Ephesians 3:18–19: "[that ye] may be able to comprehend with all saints what is the breadth, and length, and depth, and height; And to know the love of Christ, which passeth knowledge, that ye might be filled with all the fullness of God." The Apostle Paul taught with this text that the Christians of Ephesus would be filled with all the fullness of God. All the overpowering knowledge, wisdom, trust, joy, and glory of God would fill the lives of those who faithfully sought the Lord. A revival would erupt, manifesting Jesus Christ with power and virtue!

Ephesians 5:18: "And be not drunk with wine, wherein is excess; but be filled with the Spirit." This is the promise of the filling of the Holy Spirit. How the present church *needs* to be filled with the Spirit of God! Do you have any idea what it means to be full of the Spirit? Do you think it is about talking in "strange tongues," feeling chills and shivers, doing frenetic twirls, or performing the most bizarre manifestations? Dear reader, to be filled with the Holy Spirit is to be filled with God, with the third Person of the Trinity! It is to be filled with the attributes of God, the holy and irreproachable character of the divinity!

See Revelation 7:15–17: "and he that sitteth on the throne shall dwell among them. They shall hunger no more, neither thirst any more; neither shall the sun light on them, nor any heat. For the Lamb which is in the midst of the throne shall feed them, and shall lead them unto living fountains of waters." The promise to satisfy those who hunger and thirst for righteousness will not be fulfilled completely in this life. They will never be fully satisfied here, for as long as they are in the body of sin, subject to the effects of the Fall, they will continue to be hungry and thirsty.

Martyn Lloyd-Jones wrote about this: "The believer is someone who at the same time as they are hungry and thirsty, they are also being satisfied; however the more they are satisfied, the more hungry and thirsty they are."

So, the more we seek God, the more we will be satisfied; and this cycle will repeat and continue until the day we take our place in glory that was prepared for us before the foundation of the world! There, in the heavenly city, where the most perfect righteousness dwells, we will be fully accomplished, satisfied and filled with all the fullness of God, in the company of the righteous, the Lord Jesus Christ.

Conclusion

To close, I would like to challenge you with some questions: why did the Reformers turn the world upside down and give back to the people the truth of God? Why did Jonathan Edwards fire up New England with a revival? Why did David Brainerd influence thousands of missionaries with a holy zeal for God? Why was John Wesley a firebrand taken out of the fire? Why was William Carey the father of modern missions? Why did Hudson Taylor advance the kingdom of God in the interior of China? Why did Charles Studd reach the farthest parts of Africa with the banner of Christ in his hands? How did they manage to be so powerful, to live such superlative lives, and change entire nations?

It all comes down to one statement: they had hunger and thirst for God. They were satisfied because they prioritized spiritual life over all else. Just as they were satisfied, God promised that he could satisfy others, until the day of Christ's return. Dear reader, decide to seek the Lord in your generation until you are satisfied, the day when our satisfaction is complete and we are made righteous like our Lord Jesus.

CHAPTER 7

Blessed Are the Merciful

Before we move to the next beatitude, which speaks of the blessedness of the merciful, it is important to emphasize that every Christian must consciously strive to attain these characteristics more and more in their lives. This does not mean to say that achieving these goals saves us or is the basis for conversion, but rather that, because of the salvation accomplished by God's grace, the Beatitudes are benchmarks in our daily lives which show the world that we are a distinct people.

Dr. Martyn Lloyd-Jones said that the greatest tool of evangelism is the witness of the distinct life that a Christian possesses. A genuine Christian life is something extraordinary, much higher than the common standards of ethics and morality, so that the Beatitudes, and the sanctification that comes with living them, distinguish the people of God in the midst of the wicked. A distinct church points to a distinct God; a holy church points to a holy God. Therefore, a humble church of spirit, which weeps, is meek, merciful, and righteous points to a God with the same qualities, glorifying God with our testimony.

I often say that the church's gem is your holiness. This is the treasure of the church. Holiness does not only speak of being separated from what is unclean, corrupt, and immoral; it does not just talk about mortification of carnal desires. Holiness is, in addition to the separation of evil, the power that the Holy Spirit gives us to be the image of Jesus, that is, to possess unconditional love, patience, goodness, righteousness, and self-control. The more we grow in the Beatitudes and develop them, the more the holiness of Christ will shine in our lives. Robert Murray McCheyne (1813–1843) used to say that this distinctive quality of true Christians makes them "a powerful weapon in God's hands."

At this point, we come to the remarkable quality of mercy, always present in the life of the faithful followers of Jesus, reported in Matthew 5:7, "Blessed are the merciful: for they shall obtain mercy."

It is interesting to note that while the first four beatitudes deal with our relationship with God (those who are poor in spirit, who weep, who are meek, and who desire righteousness), the fifth beatitude deals with the effects of true conversion in our relationship with our neighbor and society.

Christianity is not found only within the space and parameters of corporate worship on Sunday mornings, for if it were so it would absolutely invalidate the terms taught in the New Testament which calls us to be salt of the earth and light for the lost world. Our Christianity cannot be restricted in any way to a liturgical moment, but it must be manifested in all areas of our life: business, studies, relationships, and desires. Wherever we go, wherever we walk and with whomsoever we speak, mercy must season our social relationships.

Who Are the Merciful?

What, then, is the meaning of mercy? The word mercy in this text is elleemon, derived from the Greek eleus, which expresses a feeling of compassion aroused by the misery or need of another. Therefore, to have mercy or to be merciful is to have a feeling caused by another's need or lack. In a deeper sense, it means putting yourself in the place of the other, feeling their pain. It is the compassion of the heart, which makes someone able to feel what the other person is feeling by putting themselves in their place.

Jesus said, in this beatitude, that this attribute must accompany the truly saved and therefore the church of God. If you consider yourself a Christian, you need to be merciful, feel compassion for your neighbor, put yourself in the place of your neighbor, feel their pain and their suffering, working and doing everything to alleviate their needs. Being merciful is not an option; it is a condition to be a true follower of the Lord Jesus.

This beatitude is one of those that most distinguishes the people of God from the wicked, and makes the abyss obvious between those who serve God and those who do not. The character of the wicked is marked by indifference, cruelty, perversity, coldness, intolerance, violence, revenge, selfishness, and narcissism.

John Stott (1921–2011) said that "the wicked prefer to be silent and indifferent about the suffering and misery of others, preferring revenge more than forgiveness." Why do people kill? Why do they steal, rape, and extort? Why is there so much corruption? Because of the lack of love, compassion, and mercy. Why is there a lack of mercy? Because true mercy can only exist where there is a genuine conversion! If mercy cannot be found in the world, it must be found shining brightly in the church. We must be known as the people of mercy—of compassion and goodness toward others.

Mercy is linked to empathy. Christians are not, or rather cannot be, indifferent to the suffering of others. They are the ones who feel the pain of the suffering; they cry with those who cry. There is a feeling of compassion that accompanies Christians in their daily lives, and if they encounter suffering, they will similarly feel the other person's pain. The Bible says that when Jesus performed his miracles, there was a characteristic feeling that always accompanied him: "Jesus, was moved with mercy/compassion" (see Matt 14:14, 15:32, 18:27, 20:34; Mark 14:14; Luke 7:13).

Let me ask you: are you touched by the chaos that affects so many people in Brazil? When you see the news in the media about child prostitution, pedophilia, and rape, do you feel pain? When you see the misery of northeast Brazil, the corruption of Brasilia, the millions of people unemployed, the prisoners piled up in sub-human conditions, the deaths of children, the disregard for the elderly, are you moved? Are you taken by a deep sadness? Do you find yourself in the miserable state of these creatures?

If you are insensitive to the pain and suffering of others, if you do not feel the suffering of your husband, wife, children and others around you, you need to reassess your conversion.

Mercy, besides feeling, is an attitude. There are many who are devastated by the suffering of others, then wipe away their tears and go about their day as if nothing can be done. This is not biblical mercy. Mercy is a feeling accompanied by action. There is no use having pity for a street child and then letting that child go hungry; there is no use in feeling pity for your husband and then not forgiving him; there is no use having compassion for a grandmother and only visiting her once every six months; there is no use having compassion of that blind cousin, of that crippled mother, of that brother with cancer if that feeling is not translated into an attitude and followed by action! The mercy taught by Jesus in the above texts is a feeling of compassion accompanied by practice. The Lord worked and did everything to alleviate suffering! It was as if Jesus snapped his fingers and said, "time to act." He spent his time, his sleep, his patience, his attention, and his care on those in need. He got tired, he gave of himself, and he even used his own saliva manifest God's mercy to a suffering world.

I am not saying that you will solve the problem of humanity, or that you will satisfy everyone's hunger, nor that you will open your house and fill it with beggars. I mean, if you were able to help everyone, if it was in your power, would your first feeling be compassion? If you could relieve the collective pain, would you do it? If it is impossible to solve all the problems, do you at least strive to be active where you are, attempting to relieve pain and suffering?

I am inclined to say that our generation is the most omissive in the history of Christianity. Our religion is "lab-Christianity," of Facebook, of Whatsapp, of many words and little action. There are many speculative philosophies and cogitations that do translate into practice. Our mercy has to cross borders, and reach where the needy really are! Pay attention: no one has so little that he cannot give something, and no one has so much that he cannot receive anything. You will always be able to give and always be able to receive. Perhaps you can't give a car or pay for a surgery in a private hospital for someone. However, you can give a basic food basket, you can make a visit in the hospital, and you can welcome a family for a nice meal; you can give a hug and lend your time to comfort someone, and you can buy medication in the pharmacy for that family that is not able to.

Biblical Examples of the Merciful

Now let us examine how mercy is depicted in Scripture.

First, mercy is manifested in meeting the needs of other Christians. We are not listing here the care for others in general or for the wicked, but for those who are brothers and sisters by common faith in Jesus Christ—the mercy that we exercise in relation to the people of God. The Apostle

Paul speaks about this aspect of mercy in Romans 12:13, "Distributing to the necessity of saints." The apostolic commandment in this text is that we supply the needs of the saints, that is, of those sanctified by grace: Christians. It is the duty of the faithful who are able, to supply the needs of a brother who shows a need. A true Christian, seeing his brother in need cannot deny him help.

One of the marks of the merciful is that they cannot see another brother in the faith suffering and leave him as he is. The merciful will be moved and mobilized, seeking a way of helping and supplying the beloved brother in Christ.

Galatians 6:10 says, "As we have therefore opportunity, let us do good unto all men, especially unto them who are of the family of faith." The passage says that we must do good to all men, however, there is a specification here: we must do good "especially" to those who are of the family of faith, of the people of God: that is, the pastors, clergy, deacons, musicians, brothers, sisters, new converts, and children.

See 1 John 3:17: "But whoso hath this world's good, and seeth his brother have need, and shutteth up his bowels of compassion from him, how dwelleth the love of God in him?" If anyone is able to alleviate the suffering of a faithful follower of the Lord with the resources he possesses and does not do so, how can this person have the love of Christ? The rhetorical question of the Apostle John clearly denounces that the wise must not only use words, but he must act to help the brothers and sisters around him.

Dear reader, do you care about the needs of your brothers and sisters? Do you know their needs? Do you know if there is someone in your church who is experiencing "financial hardship," some difficulty or suffering in a cause that you can help?

Could you not afford to pay for the child's or young woman's treatment in your church who cannot afford it? Couldn't you donate any of the many dresses you own for that sister who has none, or one of the many pairs of shoes to any servant of the Lord? Or perhaps you know what medication someone in the congregation uses and could alleviate that need for them?

Perhaps there are sick brothers or sisters who are hospitalized and do not have companions. Could you give up your sleep and spend the night with them, Reading the Bible, singing hymns to the Lord, and comforting them in their pain? Visit that person suffering from depression and uplifting their heart; take some groceries, eat with them, and end the visit with a word of comfort and prayer. Help that person with learning difficulty at school, who is doubtful and encourage them to continue.

The merciful one cares about the needs of his brothers and sisters in Christ; they are moved upon seeing the suffering of the saints who gather in the same place, who love the same God. They act with deep compassion, using all their ability to alleviate the problem of suffering. They cannot stand idly by, watching the pain of the saints and do nothing. If you are the kind of person who exists comfortably and lives a painless gospel, it is likely that the Lord will address your indifference to the family of faith on the day he will weigh the works of each one (1 Cor 3:10–15).

Secondly, mercy is manifested in meeting the need of the neighbor, of the wicked, and of all the people with whom we come in contact. As has been said above, in Galatians 6:10, we must also do good "to all." We demonstrate mercy when we feel compassion for all creatures, for all people, for orphanages, daycare centers, universities, prisons, asylums, dying people, beggars—of all.

There are many people who do not profess the saving faith in Christ who give enormous "lessons" to Christians in their quest for compassion and charity. They do not have eternal life, believe in so many unfounded things, but have a certain disposition, an emotion in them that impels them to do good to others. That should serve as a powerful exhortation to the church to engage with the pain and suffering of the community around it. We must never forget that the purpose of having been saved by the Lord is for us to show the world our love in selfless service to others.

Proverbs 3:28 reads, "Say not unto thy neighbor, Go, and come again, and to morrow I will give; when thou hast it by thee." If you are able to help, do not slam the door in anyone's face; do not say "I will think about it," or that they should come back later. You may never see that person again, and you will lose an excellent opportunity to manifest Christ's love in works; you will lose an opportunity to be merciful to the one who has no family, housing, or means—in short, a "piece of walking flesh" who simply expected a merciful act from the only one who can manifest true mercy: the Christian.

Again, Proverbs 25:21–22 reads, "If thine enemy be hungry, give him bread to eat; and if he be thirsty, give him water to drink: for thou shalt heap coals of fire upon his head, and the Lord shall reward thee." Here it is taught that mercy should not be directed only to others in general, but also to your enemies, even to those people who hate you and want evil for you at all cost. When your enemy is passing through a season of calamity and is suffering in crisis, it is at that time that God is saying: help him, go and help him, extend your hand to him!

Why should I exercise mercy with those who hate me? Because the impact of your attitude on the life of your enemy can lead them to repentance. It may be the instrument that God will use to convince them of their sins and to lead them to faith. Can you imagine the strength of such a testimony in the life of your enemy? This person will see the clear love of Christ shining in the form of mercy through you.

Hebrews 13:16 further raises the duty of mercy with others: "But to do good and to communicate forget not: for with such sacrifices God is well pleased." The text says that mercy is a sacrifice to God, a mild and pleasant aroma.

In Acts 10 we are told that God was pleased with the prayers and acts of mercy of the centurion Cornelius. It is said that Cornelius's charity went up as a "memorial to God" (Acts 10:4). Isn't that beggar at the traffic lights sent by God so that you have the opportunity to exercise mercy and thus make a sacrifice to God? Calling him a drug-addict, pervert, dirty, or demon-possessed does not help—he has heard this from almost all the people who have passed through there. Is not the sacrifice that the Lord expects of you to simply say to that shabby man that you care about him and are willing to alleviate his suffering however you can? I'm not saying that using mercy means taking the person to live in your house, but at least, put yourself in his place and exercise compassion.

Acts 20:35, "It is more blessed to give than to receive." When we come across a passage like this we should think: what are most of the contemporary churches doing? They are likely to be teaching their members to be self-interested, vain, concerned only with their will and desires, while the Bible teaches that Christians will be happy, complete, and joyful in giving! It is by giving that we are fulfilled, not receiving.

Our call, as God's people, is to give, to bless, and dedicate time with love for our neighbor; for this reason, sponsor the gospel, invest in actions of mercy and compassion, dress those who are naked, feed the hungry, love those who are abandoned, spend time with your neighbor!

Furthermore, mercy is demonstrated in the act of forgiveness. The merciful are not resentful, but forgive those who have offended them. The mercy taught by Jesus in this beatitude is to forgive our offenders, regardless of the offense we have suffered. See Matthew 18:21–22, "Then came Peter to him, and said, Lord, how oft shall my brother sin against me, and I forgive him? till seven times? Till seven times? Jesus saith unto him, I say not unto thee, Until seven times: but, Until seventy times seven."

In this passage, Jesus is using a hyperbole, exaggerating that if a person sins against us we should forgive them not up to a certain number of times (seven times as suggested by Peter), but as many times as necessary. It could be one hundred, two hundred, or one thousand times—every time we are reviled, because we have mercy, we must be ready to forgive. Here Jesus also teaches that forgiveness should not have a limit. There are people who forgive, "as long as," or "until." They put a limit on their forgiveness. This is not Christianity, because true religion teaches men to be unlimited in their willingness to forgive.

Matthew 6:14–15, "For if ye forgive men their trespasses, your heavenly Father will also forgive you: but if ye forgive not men their trespasses, neither will your Father forgive your trespasses." Jesus's warning is direct: the forgiveness we receive from God must follow our forgiveness to others. Without exercising mercy with others, we should not expect God to have mercy on us.

Another way we see mercy explained in Scripture shows that it is manifested in not seeking revenge. The merciful man does not expect the opportunity to avenge him who offended him. He doesn't expect the person to go through some difficulty for what he has done or to make him suffer as he suffered. Such an attitude is the fruit of the unregenerate mind, which still lives according to the standards of the flesh and not of the Spirit.

Hebrews 10:30 states, "Vengeance belongeth unto me, I will recompense, saith the Lord. And again, The Lord shall judge his people." The merciful person leaves their cause in the hands of the Lord, not seeking revenge or doing justice with their own hands. They wait upon the justice that comes from God, that he will do what is best in every cause.

James 4:11 reads, "Speak not evil one of another, brethren. He that speaketh evil of his brother, and judgeth his brother, speaketh evil of the law: but if thou judge the law, thou art not a doer of the law, but a judge." The merciful person does not undermine their neighbor; they do not speak behind their backs; they do not promote factions and riots; and they do not create situations to destroy and avenge their offender. The merciful pardon, forget, and dispel every focus of evil judgment and revenge.

We also read in Romans 12:21, "Be not overcome of evil, but overcome evil with good." The merciful do not seek revenge, but instead return good for evil. They exchange injustice with justice, resentment with love, and cruelty with kindness. The merciful portray Romans 12:10, "Be kindly affectioned one to another with brotherly love; in honor preferring one another." It is the mark of the one who is merciful to let the other side win, to let the other one be right, and to give the other the upper hand. They are not concerned with promoting themselves, with having the last word, or with proving that they're right to pay them back in the same way. They let the other have the honor.

Mercy is also manifested in evangelism. The true Christian has compassion on the condition of eternal perdition in which the wicked sinners reside. He is not indifferent to the salvation of the lost, he is empathetic; he puts himself in the place of the other, and he feels what the other feels about his state of alienation from God's forgiveness and grace. He sees the prostitutes, drug-addicts, adulterers, liars, and not only does he regard the consequences of their sinful states, but he sees the ruin they find themselves in because of their separation from God.

Augustine of Hippo (354–430) said that if you can cry for a body that dies, you should cry much more for a soul that is going to hell. Should we not be afflicted by a soul that is being condemned? Should we not cry because souls are in a state of separation from God that will lead them—sooner or later—to eternal condemnation?

The merciful are sensitive to people's need for salvation. They are passionate for souls; their great desire is to share the gospel with them, take them to the Savior, and teach them in the way of the truth. On the college campuses, they see all those well-dressed and healthy people, who seem from the outside to be happy and fulfilled, and they feel sorry for them because they are lost and without Christ; they will die at any moment, entering into eternal condemnation!

Dear reader, how long will you work or study with that person without presenting to them the holy gospel of God's glory and grace? How long will you see those people week after week and not tell them about the kingdom of God? To be merciful is to take the gospel to them and pray for them, persistently sharing until they are converted or reject the truth!

Showing mercy means saving people from suffering. When someone evangelizes they are alerting people precisely because they want to free them from eternal suffering. These people need to know that they will suffer under the wrath of God in hell, in unspeakable torment and pain, and it is the merciful one who takes to them the good news of salvation in Jesus Christ.

In Jude 1:22–23 we read, "And of some have compassion, making a difference: and others save with fear, pulling them out of the fire." Jude taught us that we should snatch up the souls that are about to be lost eternally, and by way of proclamation, prayer, and fasting, urge them to turn away from their evil ways to God.

A great example of passion for the lost in the New Testament is the Apostle Paul. See him speaking in Romans 1:14, "I am debtor both to the Greeks, and to the Barbarians; both to the wise, and to the unwise." He considered that, when he had received the gospel of God, he was a debtor to all people, obligated to share with them the same news of salvation that he had received.

He had mercy which prompted him to go out on his missionary journeys, many times risking his life and the lives of others, to preach salvation through repentance and faith in Jesus. Paul possessed so much mercy that he even said that he would rather be anathema (cursed) than to see his fellow citizens—the Jews—without salvation (Rom 9:3).

However, no mercy equates to that of Jesus Christ's for the lost. The second person of the Trinity came down from heaven with compassion for lost humanity. He left his throne to come to a world full of pain, hatred, anguish, and sin precisely to redeem those who would be eternally lost without his actions.

Matthew 9:36 reveals the mercy of Jesus for human suffering, "But when he saw the multitudes, he was moved with compassion on them, because they fainted, and were scattered abroad, as sheep having no shepherd." The crowd was exhausted, tired, lost, and careless. Jesus, seeing that they were lost, was consumed with mercy.

John 3:17 states, "For God sent not his Son into the world to condemn the world; but that the world through him might be saved." Why did Jesus not come to condemn the world? Because the world was already condemned, and men were already lost in wrongdoing and sins (Eph 2:1). The Messiah would not come to destroy what was already weak and broken. As Isaiah taught, he would not break the broken cane, nor would he wipe out the wick that was smoking (Isa 42:3). Jesus came to bestow mercy on a world that was already corrupt; his great mission was of mercy, so that the world could be saved by him.

Furthermore, mercy is a proof that attests to the salvation of a person. Remember that the mercy referred to in this beatitude is not a human quality that anyone can have or develop. It is something that only God possesses, "Be ye therefore merciful, as your Father also is merciful" (Luke 6:36); "Blessed be God, even the Father of our Lord Jesus Christ, the Father of mercies, and the God of all comfort!" (2 Cor 1:3); and "But God, who is rich in mercy, for his great love wherewith he loved us" (Eph 2:4).

Therefore, if only God has mercy, a person can receive true mercy only if the Lord gives it to him, which is what he does in someone's conversion. Only after the new birth does a person become truly merciful. Let us look at an important text on this, "For if ye forgive men their trespasses, your heavenly Father will also forgive you" (Matt 6:14).

In this passage, is Jesus teaching that God's forgiveness for my life depends on me forgiving others? No, not at all, for if this were the way of salvation, it could rest on some work that man could do, and no longer be by grace alone. What Jesus taught was that, once someone was forgiven by God and converted, it is impossible for that person not to forgive those who have offended them.

In a truly saved person, mercy is woven into their acts and values, just as the parable of Luke 10:30–33 teaches, "A certain man went down from Jerusalem to Jericho, and fell among thieves, which stripped him of his raiment, and wounded him, and departed, leaving him half dead. And by chance there came down a certain priest that way: and when he saw him, he passed by on the other side. And likewise a Levite, when he was at the place, came and looked on him, and passed by on the other side. But a certain Samaritan, as he journeyed, came where he was: and when he saw him, he had compassion on him."

Note that two highly religious people, from whom mercy was expected, did not care about the wounded man. Heed their example, reader, how easily your attitude toward others may show that the religion you profess is not the same as the one you practice with your acts! Do you not "pass by on the other side," avoid those who should be the object of your compassion? The merciful act just like that Samaritan in the parable, who was compassionate to the wounded and cared for his needs.

Blessings for the Merciful and Consequences for the Unmerciful

Continuing the analysis of the Lord's teaching, let us look below, first, at the consequences for the unmerciful and next, at the rewards of the merciful.

Proverbs 21:13 reads, "Whoso stoppeth his ears at the cry of the poor, he also shall cry himself, but shall not be heard." He who does not use mercy with those who are suffering will not receive mercy when he is suffering. Whoever is uncaring and unmerciful to those in need; the one who does not suffer with those who are suffering around them; he who does not grieve with sorrow and compassion for the pain of his loved one or neighbor: there will come the day when he will also suffer and be in distress, and no one will have mercy on him. When it is his turn to cry out, the others will also cover their ears. Simply put, those who do not exercise mercy will not receive mercy in their time of need.

Here is a biblical illustration of this truth in David's story (see 2 Sam 11–12). David stopped going to war when it was time to fight; he was idle at home, walking through his palace, when he saw a woman bathing. He discovered that she was Bathsheba, the wife of the brave warrior Uriah. He called for this woman and laid down with her, thus committing adultery. Shortly after, David discovered that the woman was pregnant. At first he devised a deceptive plan to make it appear that the child was Uriah's, and he called him back from war and gave him permission to stay with his wife.

The loyal warrior refused to rest and enjoy the company of his wife. David then offered a banquet, getting Uriah drunk so that he would lie down with his wife, but yet he refused, and stayed in David's palace. As David's plans were not working out, he sent an order to Joab, the captain of the army, to put Uriah at the harshest front of the war so that when he was fighting he would be killed; this would enable David to make his evil plan a reality, so that he could marry the widow Bathsheba, and claim the child as his own.

Everything turned out just as David planned. Uriah was killed, the war was won, Bathsheba and David got married, the baby was about to be born, the kingdom was prospering, and there was plenty of gold and prosperity; however the whole situation was "evil in the eyes of the Lord" (2 Sam 11:27).

In that period David received the visit of Nathan the prophet, who brought him a conundrum to be judged:

> There were two men in one city; the one rich, and the other poor. The rich man had exceeding many flocks and herds: but the poor man had nothing, save one little ewe lamb, which he had bought and nourished up: and it grew up together with him, and with his children; it did eat of his own meat, and drank of his own cup, and lay in his bosom, and was unto him as a daughter. And there came a traveler unto the rich man, and he spared to take of his own flock and of his own herd, to dress for the wayfaring man that was come unto him; but took the poor man's lamb, and dressed it for the man that was come to him. (2 Sam 12:1–4)

Listening to such an atrocity, David became full of indignation and anger by the evil act, and said to the prophet Nathan, "As the LORD liveth, the man that hath done this thing shall surely die. And he shall restore the lamb fourfold, because he did this thing, and because he had no pity" (2 Sam 12:5–6).

The story continued and Nathan declared that David was the man who had done that horrible thing:

Wherefore hast thou despised the commandment of the LORD, to do evil in his sight? Thou hast killed Uriah the Hittite with the sword, and hast taken his wife to be thy wife, and hast slain him with the sword of the children of Ammon. Now therefore the sword shall never depart from thine house; because thou hast despised me, and hast taken the wife of Uriah the Hittite to be thy wife. . . . the child also that is born unto thee shall surely die. (2 Sam 12:9–10, 14)

David confessed his sin, and Nathan answered that God had forgiven him, he would not die. However, his son with Bathsheba would die.

It was as if God were saying to David, "You didn't show mercy to Bathsheba, and you didn't show mercy to Uriah, so now I won't have mercy on you. You can cry, fast, and mourn, but I will judge you through this son." What was the consequence for David, who didn't show mercy? He also did not receive mercy in his despair!

Dear reader, are you suffering today, experiencing unending pain, afflictions, and hardships in which you have cried to God for mercy and your relief does not come? Are you crying to others around you for mercy, yet realizing that you are not receiving mercy and the pain does not cease?

Perhaps you are someone who has lived your whole life without showing mercy to others? Have you been negligent, omissive, blind to the suffering around you for days, months, or even years? Perhaps you could have helped someone and you didn't? You could have forgiven someone and you didn't? You could you have brought relief and you didn't? You could have ended the dispute and you didn't?

There are many who call themselves "Christians" today and live in unprecedented self-centeredness! Everything must please and benefit them. They only think of their own riches, possessions, and pleasure; everything must be geared toward meeting their narcissistic desires. I would like to say frankly that this is not the character of the true Christian.

If you have cried out and haven't received mercy today, it is very likely that you didn't show mercy when you could have. I advise you to repent, seek forgiveness from those you have offended, and then wait for God's goodness upon your life.

Now that we have examined the worldly consequences of the unmerciful, let us look at the eternal, as taught in the parable of the creditor without compassion, in Matthew 18:23–35:

> Therefore is the kingdom of heaven likened unto a certain king, which would take account of his servants. And when he had begun to reckon, one was brought unto him, which owed him ten thousand talents. But forasmuch as he had not to pay, his lord commanded him to be sold, and his wife, and children, and all that he had, and payment to be made. The servant therefore fell down,
>
> and worshipped him, saying, Lord, have patience with me, and I will pay thee all. Then the lord of that servant was moved with compassion, and loosed him, and forgave him the debt. But the same servant went out, and found one of his fellowservants, which owed him an hundred pence: and he laid hands on him, and took him by the throat, saying, Pay me that thou owest. And his fellowservant fell down at his feet, and besought him, saying, have patience with me, and I will pay thee all. And he would not: but went and cast him into prison, till he should pay the debt. So when his fellowservants saw what was done, they were very sorry, and came and told unto their lord all that was done. Then his lord, after that he had called him,
>
> said unto him, O thou wicked servant, I forgave thee all that debt, because thou desiredst me; Shouldest not thou also have had compassion on thy fellowservant, even as I had pity on thee? And his lord was wroth, and delivered him to the tormentors, till he should

pay all that was due unto him. So likewise shall my heavenly Father do also unto you, if ye from your hearts forgive not every one his brother their trespasses.

God has shown us mercy, hasn't he? He has forgiven our sins, washed us, redeemed us, and exercised great patience with the multitude of transgressions that we commit. If we do not show mercy to others—forgiving and pardoning their shortcomings—the consequence taught in the parable is to be locked in prison until all the debt is paid. The problem is that that debt is unpayable, which means that condemnation will be perpetual.

Through the work of Christ on the cross, God forgives sinners. If a person who says they are a Christian does not forgive someone who offended them, that is, does not show mercy as God has shown mercy to them, that person will be imprisoned until they pay all the debt of their sins. Because we cannot justify ourselves before God, the consequence of the lack of mercy is eternal condemnation! Therefore, if someone manifests mercy, it is evidence that they are saved. If someone does not manifest mercy, it is evidence that such a person is not saved.

Let us look at another passage that further extends the understanding of this theme in Matthew 25:41–46:

> Then shall he say also unto them on the left hand, depart from me, ye cursed, into everlasting fire, prepared for the devil and his angels. For I was an hungred, and ye gave me no meat: I was thirsty, and ye gave me no drink; I was a stranger, and ye took me not in: naked, and ye clothed me not: sick, and in prison, and ye visited me not. Then shall they also answer him, saying, Lord, when saw we thee an hungred, or athirst, or a stranger, or naked, or sick, or in prison, and did not minister unto thee? Then shall he answer them, saying, Verily

I say unto you, Inasmuch as ye did it not to one of the least of these, ye did it not to me. And these shall go away into everlasting punishment: but the righteous into life eternal.

Do you know why these people will be condemned to the eternal fire of hell? Because they did not show mercy! When those around them were in need, they did not show mercy. They no longer show mercy to a young one in the faith, to a retired and sick lady, or to their own wife for whom they vowed fidelity. When these people no longer serve the suffering who cry out, they no longer serve Christ himself, so they will go to eternal torment!

I think the most tragic text on being unmerciful is James 2:13: "For he shall have judgment without mercy, that hath shewed no mercy." The only chance that anyone on earth will be saved is if they are justified by Christ before God, because he has paid for their sins. Therefore, only if God shows someone mercy, not ascribing to them what is due because of their own sins, can this person be saved. The merits, works, and achievements of the person will not count for anything; the acquittal will depend exclusively on the mercy of the righteous Judge.

The above text teaches the judgment of the unmerciful is without mercy. Imagine if God judges them with the naked and cold sword of the Law. Could they escape? Never. Therefore, only the merciful, who were thus made known by the work of grace in their hearts, can stand before God on the last day.

Now that we have examined the consequences for the unmerciful, let's see the rewards the merciful will receive. The text in Matthew 5:7 says, "Blessed are the merciful: for they shall obtain mercy."

The first reward is mercy itself, from God due to their mercy towards others. This reward is magnificent, because we are in imminent danger of suffering: attacks by Satan, seductions of the flesh, the power of the wicked, perils of the world, and the wrath of God. In every moment, we are the targets of powers that aim to destroy us, but those who attain mercy are spared! The wrath of God—and any other danger—cannot fall upon a person who has reached the refuge, the citadel of protection of the Lord's mercy!

Secondly, the merciful will be rewarded with happiness. The Scriptures say that they are joyful and satisfied. The merciful will have hope, faith, and the security of those who have a Lawyer on the throne of the Father (1 Jn 2:1).

A third reward for those who exercise mercy will be blessedness while they are on this earth. Psalm 41:1–3 says, "Blessed is he that considereth the poor: the LORD will deliver him in time of trouble. The LORD will preserve him, and keep him alive; and he shall be blessed upon the earth: and thou wilt not deliver him unto the will of his enemies. The LORD will strengthen him upon the bed of languishing: thou wilt make all his bed in his sickness."

Have you read the tangible promises of this psalm? Did you understand the extent of God's mercy to a person who shows mercy? Do you want to enjoy these blessings? Be merciful, and God will pour upon you his blessings! God will remember you when you are sick, God will deliver you from the enemy's attack on the evil day, and God will bless you—only because you are merciful!

The promise is that you will receive relief in pain. God himself will soften your affliction! The one who gives relief to others will receive relief. Is the pain too big, is it difficult to bear? For the merciful, abundant consolations will be sent.

Fourth, the merciful will prevail in the midst of trials. Psalm 112:5–6, "A good man sheweth favor, and lendeth: he will guide his affairs with discretion. Surely he shall not be moved for ever." We cannot avoid the trials, valleys, and deserts of life, that will come, as Jesus taught: "In the world ye shall have tribulation" (Jn 16:33).

If we cannot avoid it, there is a way of going through and overcoming the difficulties: by being merciful! Those who have compassion will prevail in their trials, for God himself will defend their cause. He will be a strong tower for the merciful.

Another reward we see for the merciful is blessings upon their descendants. Psalm 37:25–26 reads, "I have been young, and now am old; yet have I not seen the righteous forsaken, nor his seed begging bread. He is ever merciful, and lendeth; and his seed is blessed." While someone who does not use mercy suffers consequences in their home while on this earth, the merciful leave as a legacy of blessings to their children.

The sixth reward for the merciful is long life from the Lord. Do you want to live a long life? Psalm 41:1–2, "Blessed is he that considereth the poor: the LORD will deliver him in time of trouble. The LORD will preserve him, and keep him alive." For the one who extends mercy, the Lord will keep him alive and deliver him from evil; this is a great mercy.

Mercy does not guarantee only earthly rewards, but also in eternal rewards. Matthew 25:34–40 states,

> Then shall the King say unto them on his right hand, Come, ye blessed of my Father! Inherit the kingdom prepared for you from the foundation of the world. For I was an hungred, and ye gave me meat: I was thirsty, and ye gave me drink:

> Naked, and ye clothed me: I was sick, and ye visited me: I was in prison, and ye came unto me. Then shall the righteous answer him, saying, Lord, when saw we thee an hungred, and fed thee? Or thirsty, and gave thee drink? When saw we thee a stranger, and took thee in? Or naked, and clothed thee? Or when saw we thee sick, or in prison,

and came unto thee? And the King shall answer and say unto them, Verily I say unto you, Inasmuch as ye have done it unto one of the least of these my brethren, ye have done it unto me.

Those who have shown mercy to their neighbor will receive from Jesus the call to participate in his eternal kingdom! He himself will say, "Come, enter the blessed rest that was prepared for you before the foundation of the world. It is for you, the merciful, the dwelling in glory. Come through the golden streets, enter the pearly gates, enjoy the new Jerusalem and have a glorified body!"

In addition to entering into the joy of the kingdom of heaven, the merciful will receive rewards in eternity. Proverbs 19:17, "He that hath pity upon the poor lendeth unto the LORD; and that which he hath given will he pay him again." When will God pay the benefit? In heaven. How will he pay? Matthew 10:42 answers this question: "Verily I say unto you, he shall in no wise lose his reward." For those who have shown mercy on earth their compassion will be remembered and rewarded in heaven.

Second Timothy 1:16–18 expresses the reward in both the earthly and the heavenly life, "The Lord give mercy unto the house of Onesiphorus; for he oft refreshed me, and was not ashamed of my chain: but, when he was in Rome, he sought me out very diligently, and found me. The Lord grant unto him that he may find mercy of the Lord in that day. And in how many things he ministered unto me at Ephesus, thou knowest very well."

Paul asked the Lord to grant mercy to a man called Onesiphorus, because during his suffering this man showed compassion to the apostle. Paul's request was twofold, both for the "house" of Onesiphorus (in the world), and in the world to come, on the last "day" (in eternity). Paul's request was that the Lord would remember with compassion the mercy shown by Onesiphorus and favor him on earth and in heaven.

James 2:13 says, "and mercy rejoiceth against judgment." However much you have sinned, however great your weaknesses may be, the Lord has promised that if you shown mercy, he himself will show mercy to you on the last day. In no way will you be condemned, because the mercy of God will triumph: it will prevail over judgment!

Conclusion

Dear reader, do you exhibit mercy in your Christian walk? Both to your brothers and sisters in Christ and to the world, do you bestow compassion that turns into action? Scripture calls Christian to show mercy in giving, forgiveness, and evangelism. The Lord has promised a great reward to those who exude mercy: unto them will mercy be returned.

CHAPTER 8

Blessed Are the Pure in Heart

After dealing with the humble in spirit, those who weep, the meek, those longing for righteousness, and the merciful, we now come to those who are clean or pure of heart, as Jesus said in Matthew 5:8, "Blessed are the pure in heart, for they shall see God." The promise of this beatitude is the greatest that a true Christian can obtain: It guarantees that the clean of heart will see God, know him, reach him, and he will make them truly complete and happy.

At this point Jesus teaches that happiness is not, as the world teaches, found in possessions, recognition, status, success, and pleasure, but rather in being filled with the fullness of God, which is the ultimate goal in the life of the Christian. Martyn Lloyd-Jones said that this is the deepest of the Beatitudes, because it carries with it the promise of knowing God in the most complete way possible to human beings.

It is important to note once again that the characteristics of the true Christian were not organized at random by Jesus in the Beatitudes. First of all, the person is poor in spirit, recognizing their misery and incapacity; then they weep, knowing that they are miserable and poor; thus they become meek, knowing they are poor, which has no merit in itself, nor is it something to boast about; for being meek, they start to hunger and thirst for righteousness, longing to be filled by God; and when they are full of the Lord, they become merciful because of the rich mercies God has lavished upon them.

Having undergone this transformation, the person is impelled to be clean of heart, because they recognize that they are not pure but rather sinful and their heart is evil; so they want to be clean of heart. Only the blessed man, who was enabled by God to recognize the evil of his own heart, cries to the Lord to cleanse him from the inside of his wickedness. This was the order that the Lord Jesus decreed in his Word.

What Does it Mean to be Pure in Heart?

Before defining the actual cleansing, let's look at the heart in context, for it is there that purity must be cultivated and blossom. Jesus taught that the first place where the Christian must be pure is in their heart.

The word heart here does not denote the organ located in the chest, responsible for pumping blood to the body; neither was Jesus referring only to human feelings, as if he was saying that blessed are those who have purity in their emotions. The heart, as it says in this passage, refers to the totality of the human being, which encompasses reason, thoughts, the will, and feelings. Thus, the totality of the affections and intentions of a Christian must be holy, pure, flowing from a clean heart, purified, and sanctified by God's presence so that the outside reflects the purity within.

Therefore, a true Christian is not pure by their practices, customs, and external action, but by the inner motivation that translates into their conduct in the outside world. Their religion does not consist of "do not do this, do not touch that, do not use this, do not practice that," but rather to do or not do something according to the purity that God has placed in the seat of their whole being—in their heart.

Proverbs 4:23 says, "Keep thy heart with all diligence; for out of it are the issues of life." Solomon was teaching, as it was common in the Hebrew culture, that the heart is the headquarters for all the inner life of man, from which come all the intents of man that lie behind the actions he takes in this world. Therefore, it is precisely there, in the heart, in the origin of the will and of its cogitations that the Christian needs to be sanctified.

Why did Jesus teach in the Sermon on the Mount about purity of the heart? Because this speech, as we have seen before, was given to the Jews, especially to many Pharisees, who had as their great idea of holiness the ceremonial cleansing, with its innumerable rituals of purification of the Law of Moses, plus those added by the commandment of the rabbis.

For example, according to the Law, a woman having her menstrual period was considered unclean and should remain separated during the period of her discharge (Lev 15:19 et seq.); the man who touched a corpse should remain separated for a certain period to be purified (Lev 19:16). Moreover, there were the purity laws taught by the rabbis, who considered someone inappropriate if they did not wash their hands to eat or did certain things on the Sabbath day (see Mark 7:5).

On account of this understanding of purity, which led to legalism and hypocrisy, Jesus taught in this beatitude that purity required by God is within, in the heart, in the hidden thoughts of man. Let us look at Jesus's criticism in Matthew 23:25–28:

> Woe unto you, scribes and Pharisees, hypocrites! for ye make clean the outside of the cup and of the platter, but within they are full of extortion and excess. Thou blind Pharisee, cleanse first that which is within the cup and platter, that the outside of them may be clean also. Woe unto you, scribes and Pharisees, hypocrites! for ye are like unto whited sepulchers, which indeed appear beautiful outward, but are within full of dead men's bones, and of all uncleanness! Even so

ye also outwardly appear righteous unto men, but within ye are full of hypocrisy and iniquity.

The second Person of the Trinity said that religion and external holiness are worthless to God. He rebuked them and called them cursed, for their cleansing did not come from a holy heart, but from outer hypocritical practices; these practices did not reflect the wickedness and perversity enclosed in their corrupt hearts. What's the use of them having outer practices that seemed just, if the intentions of their hearts were completely abominable?

Everyone could see the "clean dishes and glasses" of their religiosity and external conduct, but inside they were filled with pride, vanity, hypocrisy, covetousness and lust, greed, love of money, judgment, and hatred of others.

It is as if the Lord had said, "Inside your hearts your intentions are wrong. All you do is just for your wives to see, your work and church colleagues to see, your religious leaders to see, but your hearts are not sincere and clean before God."

When Jesus said that the Pharisees were like a whitewashed tomb, he was teaching that they were well-ornamented, beautiful, well-painted, and seemingly pure on the outside; however, what was inside the tombs? Bones, rotten flesh, worms, and vermin—all that the Jews were prevented from touching because of the order of sanctification given by God. Therefore, anyone who "touched" the Pharisees or followed their doctrine of outer holiness would in fact become unclean themselves.

Jesus spoke against this false purity in Matthew 12:34: "O generation of vipers, how can ye, being evil, speak good things? For out of the abundance of the heart the mouth speaketh." The Pharisees, despite having a corrupt heart, spoke hypocritically of good things. This accurately portrays the conduct of many today: they recite Psalms, come to services, pray for the sick, speak of the Word, express good things—but their hearts are evil, perverse, adulterous, and vengeful. They are people who take care of the outside only.

True believers are exactly the opposite: they are not concerned about saying good things, doing good things, or looking good; they are concerned about being good, being pure, and having a transformed heart. This is the true Christian. They don't care if the pastor is looking, if the husband or wife is looking, or if they are pleasing the religious elite. They don't care if the neighbors are looking. They are sincere and pure to the One who hears everything, sees everything, knows everything—they are clean in the eyes of God!

Now we can understand why Jesus made a point of qualifying the pure of heart as blessed. If the purity God analyzed was not in the intention of the heart, but rather the outside appearances, the Pharisees would definitely be in the kingdom of God. Their outward appearance was impeccable, with robes lined up, and public devotion—a model of conduct; however, when Jesus proclaimed that the purity he referred to was from the heart, none of those religious leaders would be accepted. Instead, they would be found as debtors and condemned.

Today, it is no different with the various sects and religions. Go to the Mormons, Jehovah's Witnesses, Spiritists, Buddhists, Hindus, and Muslims, whose religions are full of teachings on purification, prohibition, and forms of separation. Ask them if there is sanctification in their doctrine and you will find that there is. However, ask if there is purity of heart at the level taught by Jesus, and you will find that there is not.

What exists are several rules and standards to be followed, so that the external conduct is correct, but there is no transformation of the heart, which can only occur through conversion to the gospel of Christ and the Holy Spirit's sanctifying work in the heart of the saved. Without the inner ministry of the Spirit of God—which most of these religions deny—there is no sanctification.

Another reason for Jesus to speak in this beatitude about purity of heart is because the corruption of a man is seated in his heart. Mark 7:18–22 says,

> And he saith unto them, Are ye so without understanding also? Do ye not perceive, that whatsoever thing from without entereth into the man, it cannot defile him. Because it entereth not into his heart, but into the belly, and goeth out into the draught, purging all meats? And thus he considered all the foods pure. And he said, That which cometh out of the man, that defileth the man. For from within, out of the heart of men, proceed evil thoughts, adulteries, fornications, murders, thefts, covetousness, wickedness, deceit, lasciviousness, an evil eye, blasphemy, pride, foolishness:

The core of man's problems, his depravity, is located in his heart. It is there that the original sin lives, which was passed on to us by our first parents, Adam and Eve.

There are many philosophers and scientists who insist that the human problem is related to the environment in which they live. Therefore, they say, if human beings were taken away from the bad, evil, and sinful environment, they would improve. The Bible teaches exactly the opposite when reporting human history in Genesis 1, 2, and 3, showing that the problem is not in the environment.

Remember: Adam and Eve were in a perfect environment, where there were no sins, errors or failures; they were in the Garden of Eden, God's paradise for human beings. When they were tempted and sinned, their hearts became corrupt, despite the good environment in which they lived. Their hearts, in rebellion against God, became thirsty for every addiction, injustice, and sin.

See what Jeremiah 17:9 says, "The heart is deceitful above all things, and desperately wicked: who can know it?" Jeremiah 13:23 completes, "Can the Ethiopian change his skin, or the leopard his spots? Then may ye also do good, that are accustomed to do evil." This is the description of the human heart and the source of all evils that are manifested externally. It is not something that was placed in man externally, by nature, but a deviation from the original integrity that God gave him, so that all people are marked—including the Ethiopian with the color of his skin and the leopard with his spots—by the corruption that is within.

Returning to the text in Mark 7, we see Jesus signaling that purity must begin exactly where corruption began, that is, in the heart. The purification of the heart starts within so that the outside reflects its purity. Thus, the true Christian has their once-corrupt heart transformed and washed clean.

An important aspect to mention is that Jesus's teaching on purity of heart indicates the path to holiness. Hebrews 12:14 states, "Follow peace with all men, and holiness, without which no man shall see the Lord." However, sanctification is only possible after someone is justified by God.

All sinners have a debt with God because of the original sin they bear and the sins they commit against him. When Christ died on the cross, the transgression of the sinner which made him a debtor to God was imputed upon Christ, and his righteousness was counted as the righteousness of all those who believed. When someone repents and believes, God's "gavel" is hit in heaven, declaring that the forgiven sinner is made legally righteous.

Thus, Romans 8:1, 31–33 is fulfilled, "There is therefore now no condemnation to them which are in Christ Jesus. . . . What shall we then say to these things? If God be for us, who will be against us? He that spared not his own Son, but delivered him up for us all, how shall he not with him also freely give us all things? Who shall lay any thing to the charge of God's elect? It is God that justifieth." After the sinner's declaration of forgiveness, the process of sanctification in his life and heart begins automatically and instantly. He will no longer be common, walking like all other people who do not have a covenant with God, but will be unusual, becoming separated from sin and set apart for God, with new desires guiding his heart.

See the first truth of sanctification as a separation from sin, in 1 Thessalonians 4:3–4, "For this is the will of God, even your sanctification, that ye should abstain from fornication: that every one of you should know how to possess his vessel in sanctification and honor"; and also in 2 Corinthians 6:17–18: "Wherefore come out from among them and be ye separate, saith the Lord, and touch not the unclean thing; and I will receive you. And will be a Father unto you, and ye shall be my sons and daughters, saith the Lord Almighty."

The second truth, of sanctification for God's use is taught in 1 Peter 1:15–16, "But as he which hath called you is holy, so be ye holy in all manner of conversation; because it is written, be ye holy; for I am holy."

In this way, what is the mark of a true Christian that authenticates his life? Sanctification, which begins in all those genuinely saved, starts immediately after salvation.

Once again, it must be stressed that this is not about external sanctification, but about changing the values and desires of someone's heart. In a clean heart it is not necessary for that person's conduct to be monitored, for when they are confronted with anything or any situation that offends the holiness of God that is in them, they will walk away, so as not to displease their Lord.

For example, for the one who is clean of heart, watching something on television that goes against the desired standard of holiness for a believer cannot be tolerated; his heart will be grieved and he will abandon that television program. However, if someone says they have freedom, and are not embarrassed with scenes of immorality, sensuality and nudity, profane language, and people who take the name of God in vain, such a person does not possess freedom, but has a secret desire of being satisfied by the world and its attractions. We must not confuse the doctrine of Christian freedom—which refers to the liberty the believer has to approach the throne and worship God without earthly mediators—with the so-called freedom of some "Christians" who allow men to delight themselves with the secret passions of their hearts, putting a label of Christianity on their shameful practices.

When we advance our analysis of this beatitude, we find that the Greek term used for the word "pure" is katharos, which means generically "to purify, to clean." This is the same word used in relation to the process of purifying gold. When raw gold is extracted from nature, gold is already precious, but it is full of contamination and other metals. Gold is placed in the fire, and as the heat increases, the other metals and impurities will be separated from the gold, making that gold purified and homogeneous.

It is as if in that passage we could say that blessed are those whose hearts have no mixture, those which have gone through the process of purification and the evidences of mixtures have been erased. For this reason the religion of the Pharisees was so rebuked by Jesus, because it consisted of various doctrines, quotations, devotions, rituals, cults, and prayers that were not pure, but mixed with vanity, carnal desire, and hypocrisy. Every offering they made to God was mixed with the corruptions of their evil hearts.

In addition to the use of the word katharos for the purification of gold, we find the same term used to designate when a dirty garment had been washed. The fabric was contaminated, full of dirt, but when submitted to the washing process (purification), all residues that dirtied that tissue were removed, making the fabric clean. Another use of katharos was used to refer to wheat when it was separated from the straw that was wrapped around it. While it was mixed with straw, the wheat was not purified. Once separated from the straw, it was ready for use and was pure. Finally, the Greek term was also used to classify a "chosen/purified" army, from which soldiers who had no capacity to fight had been separated—for being fearful, faltering, or discontent—forming a homogeneous, solid, and battle-ready group.

We can see that Jesus was teaching something very specific here: blessed was the one in whose heart there were no competing loyalties. People whose heart was free from contamination, completely consecrated to God; people whose heart was not taken by the cares of this world, but who were restored from their fallen state to a state of grace before God.

Ecclesiastes 7:29, "Lo, this only have I found, that God hath made man upright; but they have sought out many inventions." In the original Creation of God, Adam and Eve had a heart like this one, which was right, pure towards God, wishing to obey and honor him above all. With the Fall in sin, their hearts were contaminated, and they became lovers of themselves and were concerned with their own satisfaction rather than satisfying the Lord.

Therefore, before conversion, the heart of man is full of idols, passions and desires that are in rebellion against God. John Calvin (1509–1564) said that the heart of man is an idol factory. Therefore, in order to have a pure heart, man needs his heart to be restored to the original state, which occurs with conversion. Let us look at God's promise in Ezekiel 36:24–25: "For I will take you from among the heathen, and gather you out of all countries, and will bring you into your own land. Then will I sprinkle clean water upon you, and ye shall be clean: from all your filthiness, and from all your idols, will I cleanse you."

When someone is converted, God removes the mixtures of their heart, the idols, vanities, hypocrisy, and worldly anxieties, creating a pure untainted heart, which is not divided and where there is deep desire for God. The heart becomes exclusive to God, and is no longer tainted by the passions that previously dominated them so much.

I confess, dear reader, that this was one of the beatitudes that challenged me the most. As I studied it and meditated on it in prayer, I said to the Lord, "I still have some loyalties competing in my heart; I still have some idols to get rid of. My heart is not pure as it should be. It still has reserves, impediments, and fears; it still has other sources and other resources that are not the Lord."

True Nature of the Pure in Heart

How many are pure in their hearts? How many read the Scriptures hoping to meet with God? Pray to him wholeheartedly? Who go to a service like a child, only to worship the Lord? How many utter praises from their mouths that truly reflect their hearts?

For us to understand, dear reader, a clean heart is one that is not divided, that is devoid of contamination; it is pure and upright. It is a completely different heart from the one that Jesus spoke about in Matthew 15:7–9, "Ye hypocrites! Well did Isaiah prophesy of you, saying, this people draweth nigh unto me with their mouth, and honoureth me with their lips; but their heart is far from me. But in vain they do worship me, teaching for doctrines the commandments of men."

If the heart is not entirely subject to God, we can worship him externally, but we worship him in vain, as a mechanical act and not purely and completely, as he requires. This outward worship, with other passions that divide the heart, is reprimanded by God in Amos 5:21–23: "I hate, I despise your feast days, and I will not smell in your solemn assemblies. Though ye offer me burnt offerings and your meat offerings, I will not accept them: neither will I regard the peace offerings of your fat beasts.

Take thou away from me the noise of thy songs; for I will not hear the melody of thy viols."

Why did God not receive the worship and devotional acts of that people? Because they did not come from pure, sincere, and broken hearts. All the outer acts did not represent anything in the holy and pure eyes of God, who expected the devotion from the heart.

Psalm 24:3–4 questions, "Who shall ascend into the hill of the LORD? Or who shall stand in his holy place? He that hath clean hands, and a pure heart; who hath not lifted up his soul unto vanity, nor sworn deceitfully." Who can dwell with God? Who can be in his holy presence? He who does not have competing loyalties in his heart, who is free from mixture, who does not give his life over to sin.

Let us look at the prayer of someone who wished to be pure in his heart in Psalm 86:11, "Teach me thy way, O Lord; I will walk in thy truth: unite my heart to fear thy name." Such a person cries out for the Lord would take control, fill them with the desire to be pure to God; they did not want to love or share God with anything else.

A powerful test to know if someone's heart is really pure and God-focused is taught by Jesus in Matthew 6:19–23:

> Lay not up for yourselves treasures upon earth, where moth and rust doth corrupt, and where thieves break through and steal; but lay up for yourselves treasures in heaven, where neither moth nor rust doth corrupt, and where thieves do not break through nor steal: For where your treasure is, there will your heart be also. The light of the body is the eye. If therefore thine eye be single, thy whole body shall be full of light. But if thine eye be evil, thy whole body shall be full of darkness. If therefore the light that is in thee be darkness, how great is that darkness!

How do we know where our treasure is? For where it is will be our heart, our desire. Now, how do we know where the heart is? Through the eyes; the pure of heart have their eyes fixed on God, focused on him. When Jesus said "if your eyes are good," he was stating that if our eyes are focused on God, "your whole body will light up [it will have light]," that is, we will be pure in heart.

In the present text, the focus is not the "eye" as an organ, but rather the goal, the objective, i.e. vision in general. Jesus established simply that if our desire is in the passions of this world, we will have a life full of darkness and we will not have a clean heart. However, if our desires are set on the glory of God and on his kingdom, we will have light.

I would like to give an example here. I work in a church as the main pastor and in the full-time management of a missionary society. My office is full of several study Bibles and thousands of books. I provide counsel to people daily, prepare sermons, write, answer letters and e-mails, and deal with a very tight schedule of commitments and invitations; in short, it is a day all possessed by God's work. Even so, my eyes may not be set on God!

My thoughts may be on the offerings my ministry receives, on praise, on the number of attendees at a service, on fame, popularity, on books sold, on the recognition received, to name a few. I can be surrounded by the things of God, but with my eyes completely in darkness, far from him! Therefore, my constant prayer and vigilance is that people may not see me, my work or my ministry, but Christ, the exalted Lamb of God, who must be crowned and blessed!

Why are many ministers involved in God's work being condemned? They work for the treasures of the world and not for the treasures of heaven. They try to serve God while serving themselves—they are serving two masters! They have loyalties that compete in their hearts, so they are divided, mixed, and not pure of heart.

Something that needs to be clear in the days in which we live is that the true Christian must first seek the will of God revealed in his Word for every specific situation in their life. This is taught in Matthew 6:33, "But seek ye first the kingdom of God, and his righteousness; and all these things shall be added unto you."

The true Christian must ask these questions, "In this purchase that I intend to make, what is the will of God? In this meeting I will have, how can the kingdom of God come first? How will I honor God's righteousness first with this money that I possess? How am I seeking the kingdom of God in this trip that I intend to make? Is the way I care for my family consistent with putting God's righteousness first? Is the way I act in evangelizing the lost and edifying the converted in line with the order to seek first the kingdom of heaven?"

The pure of heart no longer love the riches of this life more than God. They are content with what they have. They do not live to possess more and more possessions, as Paul taught in 1 Timothy 6:7–8, "For we brought nothing into this world, and it is certain we can carry nothing out. And having food and raiment let us be therewith content."

These blessed people, who have been made clean of heart, are those for whom the presence and fellowship with God are available. Only one whose heart is purified to God has their prayers answered by the Lord (see Jn 15:7). Many pray, ask the Lord for things, cry out to be filled with the Holy Spirit, but never get what they ask for in their prayers, because their hearts are divided—they have conflicting loyalties within themselves.

This statement is made in James 4:8, "Draw nigh to God, and he will draw nigh to you. Cleanse your hands, ye sinners; and purify your hearts, ye double minded." The text teaches that we must go to God, seek him, so that he may reveal himself more and more to us. However, in this approach, the person needs to be purified in their hands—outside—and in their heart, leaving their double mindedness, that is, the vacillations of desires that are competing for the willpower of this person.

Once again, as we have seen above in Psalm 24, we are taught that the one who ascends into the hill of the Lord, who enters his holy place, who has fellowship with God, is the one who has "clean hands," speaking of external sanctification, and "pure heart," that is, who has a heart without divisions or rivalries against God.

Dear reader, I would like you to go back to your conversion and first love—that sweet state in which your heart completely belonged to the Savior, in which pleasing him was your main goal and enjoying him your great desire. That time when the Lord was your "pearl of great value," your "hidden treasure," and the "most desired among the thousands" in your soul. Leave the vanities that divide your heart, abandon your double mindedness, turn entirely to the Lord, and you will find joy like you experienced at the beginning of your walk with Christ.

2 Timothy 2:22 says, "Flee also youthful lusts. But follow righteousness, faith, charity, peace, with them that call on the Lord out of a pure heart." Paul was teaching his disciple not to have idols in his heart that rival with God, for the only way that Timothy could be approved in his devotion would be to grow in the virtues that the apostle quoted, becoming clean of heart, just like all those who invoked the Lord.

Jeremiah 29:13 says, "And ye shall seek me, and find me." When do you find God? "When ye shall search for me with all your heart." That means wholeheartedly! There are many who pray to the Lord, who ask him for his presence and fellowship, but there at the bottom of the heart they continue to nourish a forbidden passion for some man or woman, a hidden covetousness, rooted selfishness, or a willingness to do God's will only to the extent that it does not conflict with one's own interests. The Lord requires us to seek him at whatever cost, having abandoned all former desires.

Biblical Examples of the Pure in Heart

Next we will take a look at some examples of those in Scripture who were pure in heart.

Psalm 73:25: "Whom have I in heaven but thee? And there is none upon earth that I desire beside thee." What a beautiful declaration of Asaph—a man who had a heart completely turned to God. He did not possess or worship any other than Yahweh. There was no reservation in his being, but he was totally devoted to the Lord!

Psalm 40:8: "I delight to do thy will, O my God: yea, thy law is within my heart." What joy and contentment it was for David, pure of heart, to know the will of God and practice it. Only someone who had nothing rivalling the holiness of God could have so much pleasure in the Lord.

However, if we look at Psalm 51:11 we are even more amazed at David's sincere desire: "Cast me not away from thy presence; and take not thy holy spirit from me." David wrote this Psalm after he sinned miserably with Bathsheba and treacherously killed her husband, the brave Uriah. How does this show someone who is pure of heart? Committing mistakes, having sins and failures, does not imply the impossibility of someone being clean of heart. With David's statement in this psalm we clearly see that his great concern, even though he had sin, was not to lose the presence of God and his Holy Spirit. David's heart was not focused on the loss of the kingdom of Israel, of the army, on the loss of gold, of reputation, or of other women; his great concern was about losing the Lord, which he could not bear!

It was as if David had cried out with this psalm, "Lord, my heart is yours, I have only eyes for you, I have no treasure besides you. Please don't take that from me, don't let me out of your blessed presence!" Here's the clean heart!

As a last example, let's refer to a few scriptural descriptions of the Lord Jesus, which show his will with total devotion to the Father, without reservations, without loyalties fighting for his attention, and without any pretense of asserting himself. The Lord had as his sole goal to do the complete will of him who sent him, thus becoming the great example to be followed by the pure of heart. John 6:38, "For I came down from heaven, not to do mine own will, but the will of him that sent me."

Paul writes biographically about Jesus in Philippians 2:5–11:

> Let this mind be in you, which was also in Christ Jesus: who, being in the form of God, thought it not robbery to be equal with God; but made himself of no reputation, and took upon him the form of a servant, and was made in the likeness of men; and being found in fashion as a man, he humbled himself, and became obedient unto death, even the death of the cross. Wherefore God also hath highly exalted him, and given him a name which is above every name, That at the name of Jesus every knee should bow, of things in heaven, and things in earth, and things under the earth, and that every tongue should confess that Jesus Christ is Lord, to the glory of God the Father.

Can you see the Master as totally clean of heart, without any remnant, detriment, or idol in his devoted heart? He lived absolutely focused on God.

I sincerely pray that the Savior generates that same heart in you. Moreover, this was David's request in Psalm 51:10, "Create in me a clean heart, O God; and renew a right spirit within me." May God grant you an inclined will—in its completeness—for him and his Word. May the

Lord put in your heart the desire to obey him in everything, even if it means losing everything, people, and the comforts of this world. May your joys be found in God, with no other trivialities competing for his affection. May having God, through Jesus Christ, be the rhythm of the new heartbeat that you have received from the Lord.

After analyzing in detail what it means to be pure in heart, we need to conclude with the promise of this unique beatitude. The reward for the clean of heart, those who guard themselves from evil, who have an innocent, naive, simple and righteous heart toward the Lord is nothing more and nothing less than "they will see God" (Matt 5:8). With absolute certainty, this is the greatest desire of a true Christian: to see God.

While there is the future aspect of this reward, of seeing God in heaven in eternity, there is also the aspect of seeing God as we walk in the flesh, in this life under the sun. Of course, this promise does not speak of a physical vision of God. We cannot see God, because he is not a physical body—he is not matter; God is Spirit (Jn 4:24). The "see" promised here concerns a greater manifestation of God, knowing him more deeply, having greater intimacy with him. This remarkable reward is only reserved for the pure in heart.

This point is very related to Mark 10:15: "Verily I say unto you, whosoever shall not receive the kingdom of God as a little child, he shall not enter therein." A child is not pure or innocent simply because he is a child. A child is born with sin in his heart and needs the same salvation as an adult. The point Jesus defended is that a child is more trusting; she has a heart much more inclined to faithfully believe in what is said to her than someone older. A child is not yet immersed in the malice that characterizes much of the adult life. Thus, we can conclude that those who will see God are those who have their hearts cleansed from idols that conflict with the Lord. You enter the kingdom and find joy in the Lord when you pray as a child, read the Scriptures as a child, and worship and adore God as a child!

Below, let's see some biblical examples of people who saw God, contemplated his holy presence, and were transformed by this vision.

Consider Moses's case:

> And the LORD said unto Moses, I will do this thing also that thou hast spoken: for thou hast found grace in my sight, and I know thee by name. And he said, I beseech thee, shew me thy glory. And he said, I will make all my goodness pass before thee, and I will proclaim the name of the LORD before thee; and will be gracious to whom I will be gracious, and will shew mercy on whom I will shew mercy. And he said, Thou canst not see my face: for there shall no man see me, and live. And the LORD said, behold, there is a place by me, and thou shalt stand upon a rock. And it shall come to pass, while my glory passeth by, that I will put thee in a clift of the rock, and will cover thee with my hand while I pass by. And I will take away mine hand, and thou shalt see my back parts: but my face shall not be seen. (Exod 33:17–23)

> And the LORD descended in the cloud, and stood with him there, and proclaimed the name of the LORD. And the LORD passed by before him, and proclaimed, The LORD, the LORD God, merciful and gracious, longsuffering, and abundant in goodness and truth; keeping mercy for thousands, forgiving iniquity and transgression and sin, and that will by no means clear the guilty; visiting the iniquity of the fathers upon the children, and upon the children's children, unto the third and to the fourth generation! And Moses made haste, and bowed his head toward the earth, and worshipped. (Exod 34:5–8)

Here is a man who saw God. Moses had just left Egypt, after his people suffered four hundred and thirty years of slavery in that land. God performed miracles and wonders there that he never did again in any other place or time. Moses contemplated the supernatural with a poignancy that no one had ever contemplated. In the texts above, we see him dissatisfied, arguing with God that his great desire had not yet been met. He implored, begged to see God. He wanted to see the glory of God.

In view of this request, the Lord told him that he would put him in the slit of a rock and pass by him with his glory, so that Moses would see his back, that is, the most that a man could bear to see. God passed by him and proclaimed his name to him, marking Moses so intensely with this experience that when he came down from Mount Sinai and presented himself to the multitude of Israelites, they could not look at Moses's face, because it shone with such a strong light that it overshadowed them.

This episode occurred when Moses was more than eighty years old. He had already been stripped of the riches he'd inherited Egypt. He was humiliated and dispossessed of the vanities of this world, having humbly taken care of the flock of his father-in-law Jethro in isolation. The impurities and idols of Moses's heart had already been dissolved by the many years of God's treatment in his life, so much so that Moses wanted no other than God. Surely Moses was the greatest figure in the Old Testament. It is rare to see someone who gave himself so much to God and his cause as Moses, the man who so loved God, who saw him as no other had seen.

We now come to John the Baptist, in John 1:29–34,

The next day John seeth Jesus coming unto him, and saith, Behold the Lamb of God, which taketh away the sin of the world! This is he of whom I said, After me cometh a man which is preferred before me: for he was before me. And I knew him not: but that he should be made manifest to Israel, therefore am I come baptizing with water. And John bare record, saying, I saw the Spirit descending from heaven like a dove, and it abode upon him. And I knew him not: but he that sent me to baptize with water, the same said unto me, upon whom thou shalt see the Spirit descending, and remaining on him, the same is he which baptizeth with the Holy Ghost. And I saw, and bare record that this is the Son of God.

John the Baptist did not know Christ; he did not know who he was. When Jesus walked to the Jordan River, John the Baptist had a revelation shown to him by the Spirit revealing this Messiah. But, who is Jesus? God manifested in human form, the exact expression of the Lord in the second person of the Trinity (Heb 1:3). God revealed to John the Baptist who he was in the person of his Son, so he could contemplate the divinity of Jesus.

Until then many thought that Jesus was an exceptional man, a prophet, a personality; but John the Baptist, because he was pure of heart, had the revelation that he was the Lamb of God, the one who would atone for the sin of humankind perfectly! How do we know that John the Baptist was pure of heart? Just return to John 1:19–26, where we can see him answering the Jews who questioned his John's identity, affirming that he was not the Christ, Elijah, or the prophet; rather John was a humble servant, who baptized with water, waiting for Him who would baptize with the Holy Spirit (Jn 1:33). John was someone who had a simple and pure heart, who worshiped only the Lamb, only the Lord.

John the Baptist, clean of heart and poor in spirit, had practical purity—he lived in the desert, and fed himself on locusts and wild honey. He was humble and not self-exalting; he only sought the Lord. Those like John the Baptist are the ones who see God. They are the pure ones, the ones who do not set their hearts on things of this world; they are loyal only to the Lord.

We can conclude from Scripture that during the thirty years that Jesus had already been on the earth, John the Baptist had not yet seen him. During this time what was John the Baptist doing? Avoiding idols, and purifying and sanctifying himself—looking for the Messiah to come. Then what happened: one day, in the Jordan River, he saw the holy Lamb of God!

Let us now look at the disciples Peter, James, and John in Matthew 17:1–2: "And after six days Jesus taketh Peter, James, and John his brother, and bringeth them up into an high mountain apart. And was transfigured before them: and his face did shine as the sun, and his raiment was white as the light." That place where the disciples were with Jesus was called the Mount of the Transfiguration. Jesus had a physical body like ours: so he bled when he got a cut, he was tired, felt hunger and exhaustion, wore normal clothes, and had dirty feet after travelling through the dust. But on this particular event, he ascended a hill and showed his divine glory to the disciples—that was the transfiguration.

Those who accompanied him were Peter, James, and John, the disciples of the Jesus's inner circle. These were the men who left everything to follow Jesus: their homes, families, professions, dreams, and comfort. They put off their former lives, and all they did was live with and follow Jesus wherever he went. On the day narrated in the passage above, Jesus took the three disciples—perhaps the purest of the large group—and manifested to them his glory. They saw God! It was worth all the separation and everything they'd lost, so that they could win the greatest prize: seeing God!

Finally, let's take a look at the last apostle to live: John—old and imprisoned because of his testimony of the gospel on the island of Patmos:

> And I turned to see the voice that spake with me. And being turned, I saw seven golden candlesticks and in the midst of the seven

candlesticks one like unto the Son of man, clothed with a garment down to the foot, and girt about the paps with a golden girdle. His head and his hairs were white like wool, as white as snow; and his eyes were as a flame of fire; and his feet like unto fine brass, as if they burned in a furnace; and his voice as the sound of many waters. And he had in his right hand seven stars: and out of his mouth went a sharp two-edged sword. And his countenance was as the sun shineth in his strength. And when I saw him, I fell at his feet as dead. And he laid his right hand upon me, saying unto me, Fear not; I am the first and the last I am he that liveth, and was dead; and, behold, I am alive for evermore, Amen; and have the keys of hell and of death. (Rev 1:12–18)

John saw God; he really saw him! He contemplated him in a wonderful vision. Imagine the warmth the apostle felt, all alone with an old heart, as he remembered seeing the Master who had ascended to heaven so many years before. What memories, what tenderness, what satisfaction, what joy and comfort it must have been for the Apostle John to have seen, in his glorified state, the Lord he had followed on earth.

The Bible says that John was the disciple whom Jesus loved, who reclined upon the bosom of the Lord, which shows John's intimacy with Jesus and, above all, where his heart was. He was a close disciple of the Lord, pure in heart, in the sense that there were no idols in his heart.

Dear reader, these examples of people who have seen God are part of a very select group in Scripture. They are people who have been graced by the Lord because of their complete devotion to him. We know that salvation is not by works, so do not misunderstand: I am teaching that, in the light of their search, these people have been favored with something sublime, being able to contemplate a little of God's glory while in this fallen world. Don't be fooled, you will receive this reward if you are free from all of the shame that surrounds you, wholly devoting yourself to the Lord, with all your heart.

If this occurs for you, be sure, you will never be the same again. When you read Isaiah 6, you will see that the prophet was never the same person again after having had a glimpse of God's majesty. When Isaiah saw the Lord, he declared that he was perishing. An angel touched his lips with a live coal from the altar of God, purifying him. Soon after, he heard God's voice asking who would take his message to his people. After being purified and seeing God—and only after this—Isaiah was one of the greatest prophets of all time, all due to the vision of God he had received.

Conclusion

If you wish to be used by Lord, you will need to be clean of heart. To walk along this path, you will have to tear down the idols in your heart, give yourself totally to God, relyng on him alone. I'm not telling you to stop working or studying, or to abandon your responsibilities. I am telling you to have a new passion and direction in your heart, so that you may belong only to the Lord.

A verse that must be mentioned is 2 Corinthians 3:18: "But we all, with open face beholding as in a glass the glory of the Lord, are changed into the same image from glory to glory, even as by the Spirit of the Lord."

What does this text say? It refers to Moses on Mount Sinai, when he saw the glory of God and put a veil before his face. Today, the Apostle Paul says, the veil is removed by the grace and manifestation of Christ, providing a progressive knowledge of God. Today, we do not have the glorious manifestations like those of the Old Testament, the so-called theophanies, which were amazing appearances of God. I admit that I personally would like to have seen them, but that is not how the Lord reveals himself today.

For us under the new covenant, we have the greatest revelation of God given to men: the person of Christ and his gospel. Therefore, to see God is to have an even greater vision of the Lord Jesus, to grow in his knowledge, to approach and have intimacy with God—all of which is accomplished through the Holy Spirit. "From glory to glory" means that as I purify myself, as I separate myself from the world, I will then come closer to God, I will know the Lord more, and he will reveal himself more to my mind and heart until I come to see him through the eyes of faith. This can occur as you read the Scriptures and pray to him throughout your day and the good and bad circumstances of your life. Be pure in heart and the Lord will meet you, revealing himself to you.

The second aspect of the reward for the clean of heart is to see God in heaven. 1 John 3:2 states, "But we know that, when he shall appear, we shall be like him; for we shall see him as he is." In heaven we will see the person of God as much as possible. This reward will be—as will the rest of the Beatitudes—finally fulfilled in the life of true Christians when they enter eternity and meet with the Lord.

CHAPTER 9

Blessed Are the Peacemakers

Before we examine another quality that marks the life of a true Christian, let's remember how these Beatitudes prove the effectiveness of Christ's sacrifice. When we read Titus 2:14, we find the answer to why Jesus came to offer himself as a sacrifice, die, and rise again: "[Jesus] gave himself for us, that he might redeem us from all iniquity, and purify unto himself a peculiar people, zealous of good works." What are these good works? The Beatitudes.

Christ's work at Calvary was not just to take us out of sin and grant us eternal life, but also involved the transformation of our character, planting within us the seeds that would grow into fruits that accompany conversion. Therefore, when we manifest meekness, purity of heart, mercy, and humbleness of spirit, we are showing the Beatitudes in good works, that is, proving the effectiveness of Christ's sacrifice, as Paul said to Titus.

Jesus said in Matthew 5:9, "Blessed are the peacemakers: for they shall be called children of God." What did Jesus mean by the term "peacemaker"? What does being a peacemaker entail? It is a characteristic of the true servant of the kingdom of God, who possesses both internal peace and actively promotes it between others and the world around them; they show peace wherever they go, even when approaching enemies, being authentic ambassadors of peace.

Where there is a chaotic environment, the peacemaker, with their presence, words, and actions, restores peace and untangles confusion and disorder. The true Christian brings and promotes reconciliation.

Now, do you know what might be surprising today? Where there is a dispute, there is often a "Christian" involved! Amidst the disorder, there is the "Christian," speaking vulgarly, spreading rumors, gossiping, and rebelling, thus demonstrating that there is no true Christianity in their life, rather a dead religiosity that does not imitate Jesus Christ. There are "brothers and sisters" who by their simple presence promote strife, anger, division, and discord. This leads me to ask: how can the Spirit of the living God dwell in people like these?

We need to understand urgently that when a Christian is pressed, what must come out of them is kindness, politeness, and peace, just as when an orange tree is shaken and oranges fall out. However, if the Christian is confronted with contention and arguments, we may see that the fruits they produce are not in accordance with the faith they profess, such as if an orange tree is shaken and lemons fall out; there is something wrong with that tree.

The word peace is used in Scripture in two ways, both passively and actively. Passively, it describes an internal condition of the individual, such as the expression we use in English "peace of mind." It is used by Jesus in John 14:27a, "Peace I leave with you, my peace I give unto you." This is an internal state of tranquility—mature trust in the salvation of Christ, in the reconciliation and adoption of God, and in the possession of the certainty that the guilt of sin was removed. In this regard, one who has inner peace has the security of salvation and of the continuing work of the Holy Spirit in them to keep them persevering to the end.

The active meaning of the word peace is found in the Greek word that Jesus employs for "peacemakers" (eirenopoios) in Matthew 5:9, which can be translated as "the one who makes peace." It is not only he who feels peace, but he who sends peace, promotes peace, and distills peace. This is not something passive, but active. The genuine Christian is a peacemaker in all areas of society: from the inner sanctum of the home to the border of an enemy nation.

A nuance of peace referred to in this beatitude that should be mentioned is that it points to the model of Christ. A peacemaker is similar to him. See Colossians 1:18–20, "And he [Jesus] is the head of the body, the church: who is the beginning, the firstborn from the dead; that in all things he might have the preeminence. For it pleased the Father that in him should all fullness dwell; and, having made peace through the blood of his cross, by him to reconcile all things unto himself; by him, I say, whether they be things in earth, or things in heaven."

Jesus, through his blessed work, made peace between God and men, reconciling two parts which, because of human sin and divine holiness, could not be brought closer unless a mediator was interposed. Jesus was this mediator, this ambassador of peace, who restored the relationship between God and man.

Ephesians 2:14–18 teaches more about the great Peacemaker:

For he is our peace, who hath made both one, and hath broken down the middle wall of partition between us; having abolished in his flesh the enmity, even the law of commandments contained in ordinances; for to make in himself of twain one new man, so making peace; and that he might reconcile both unto God in one body by the cross, having slain the enmity thereby. And came and preached peace to you which were afar off, and to them that were nigh. For through him we both have access by one Spirit unto the Father.

Who has made enmity between two irreconcilable peoples? Jesus! It was he who righted wrongs and promoted peace. In the Jewish mentality of the time, the Jews considered themselves the chosen people of God—and indeed they were—but they did not use their election to shine the light of God into the lost world or to serve as benchmarks for other nations to seek God. They boasted the fact that they were God's chosen people to spite others, to judge them and live a life of blatant sin against the God whom they said they served (see Romans 2 on this aspect).

What did Jesus do? By proclaiming the gospel, dying on the cross and rising from the dead, he established his kingdom, placing both Jews and Gentiles in the same church. He was prepared to break down enmity, diffuse the struggle, and promote the alliance. It is as if Christ had said, "They will be one people, they will have to gather together, they will have to be called Christians, they will have lunch and dinner together. . . . and I will be the one to promote that peace!"

Dear reader, when someone asks about you, wondering about your behavior, what will they learn? What if we asked this question to your wife or husband? To your mother and your father? To your children? To your boss or to your employees? To school or work colleagues? Would they respond that you are a man or woman who promotes peace? Would you say that you are someone of peace who does not engage in contentions or dissensions, but who always seeks reconciliation?

In our homes, tensions abound. Everything may seem peaceful and harmonious from the outside, but inside the walls, strife and unrest exists in the family, whether that be between husband and wife or parents and children. However, in our world, chaos reigns. When we remember the wars and unrest in our past and today, it leads us to wonder: why are there so many wars if we are living in the period of greatest technological and "human" advance of all time? How many conflicts, deaths and violence! All attempts to promote peace, reconciliation and harmony are invariably frustrated, because anger and violence are caused by sin. Something that the fallen world will never understand is that the corruption of the heart of man brings conflict.

We need to understand that what makes man quarrelsome and confrontational is not the place in which he is situated. If the human environment is transformed and it has access to the right resources and culture, can it be changed into something better? No, it cannot. It is not environment or resources that make people bad, but quite the opposite: it is men and women who corrupt the world around them. Change does not need to be social, cultural, economic or political in order for the world to improve, because the problem is in the corrupt human heart, it is in the root of Adam— the radical depravity of man!

Therefore, the only institution that can promote true peace is the church, because only the church is the bearer and preacher of the gospel (1 Tim 3:14–16), which has the power to transform the human heart. Only Christians can be peacemakers, because they are those who have been reconciled with God through the blood of Jesus. They have peace with God and a regenerated heart that can promote reconciliation in the world. Therefore, only the gospel of peace (Eph 6:15) can promote peace in the world through the church.

True Nature and Biblical Examples of a Peacemaker

Now let's examine how to identify a peacemaker. First, we recognize a peacemaker by their inner quietude. This quietude comes due to the certainty of the peacemaker that they were reconciled with God (Rom 8:16). They have this peace even in the midst of tribulations. They do not lose their peace of mind, even in the most terrible adversity.

Note the example of David in Psalm 3:1–5: "LORD, how are they increased that trouble me! Many are they that rise up against me. Many there be which say of my soul, there is no help for him in God. But thou, O LORD, art a shield for me; my glory, and the lifter up of mine head. I cried unto the LORD with my voice, and he heard me out of his holy hill. I laid me down and slept; I awaked; for the LORD sustained me!"

David was being hunted by Saul, pledged to be killed, and was under unrelenting persecution and much suffering. How did the peacemaker David respond in such an alarming situation? He said the Lord was his shield and his glory. He said he could lie down and sleep because God supported him. He laid down and slept even under Saul's persecution. Even while suffering he enjoyed peace! The peacemaker rests on God's sovereignty and his tender love for him.

2 Corinthians 4:8–9 tells the account of another peacemaker: "We are troubled on every side, yet not distressed; we are perplexed, but not in despair; persecuted, but not forsaken; cast down, but not destroyed." The Apostle Paul is giving a description of the ministers of God, missionaries, and holy martyrs of the early church who suffered all these things.

How did they respond? They did not lose their balance, they did not leave the church, they did not stop reading the Word of God, they did not abandon prayer, they did not quit the fight against sin. They did not fail to trust in the divine promises. Even under Jewish persecution and the Roman sword—look at this beautiful peace! Such an account seems like a lie in the present day! They were afflicted, but the tribulation was not greater than the God who sustained them; although they were impacted by what God had allowed to happen to them, they were not discouraged. They were persecuted, but they always had a way out, a refuge; they were downcast many times, but they were always visited by God's supernatural power in their soul, being renewed and made bold as lions (Prov 28:1).

Secondly, we recognize a peacemaker who does not strike back when attacked. Romans 12:19–21 teaches, "avenge not yourselves, but rather give place unto wrath: for it is written, vengeance is mine; I will repay, saith the Lord. Therefore if thine enemy hunger, feed him; if he thirst, give him drink: for in so doing thou shalt heap coals of fire on his head. Be not overcome of evil, but overcome evil with good."

The peacemaker does not seek revenge, does not enact justice with their own hands, does not accept provocation, and does not strike back when attacked. Now, would there be room in Christianity for a "vindictive Christian" who paid back evil with evil? The peacemaker returns the evil they received not with evil intentions, but with good. Note that the peacemaker portrayed in this passage was offended, mistreated, betrayed and oppressed, but he did not take the matter into his own hands, seeking revenge!

Matthew 5:39–40, "But I say unto you, That ye resist not evil: but whosoever shall smite thee on thy right cheek, turn to him the other also. And if any man will sue thee at the law, and take away thy coat, let him have thy cloak also." Jesus is teaching that if you were wounded on one cheek, you must be willing to turn the other cheek. At this point we ask God, "Why?" Because the Christian is a peacemaker, so it is not in his new heart to strike back.

Every mature Christian knows that, when he decided to forget this principle and to strike back, revenge brought only upheaval, war, strife, and much sadness. Because they are peacemakers, Christians know that they have not been regenerated from on high to take part in fights like these. They are convinced that they are in this world to promote peace, so they willingly seek not to strike back when attacked.

Third, we recognize peacemakers by their words. Being a peacemaker is a quality of one who has a transformed heart, born again. Matthew 12:34 states, "O generation of vipers, how can ye, being evil, speak good things? For out of the abundance of the heart the mouth speaketh." Words reflect the heart, so only someone who has been regenerated can truly speak of peace and reconciliation.

Proverbs 15:1 teaches, "A soft answer turneth away wrath: but grievous words stir up anger." The peacemaker is the only one capable of having the soft answer, the one that turns away wrath and promotes peace. Every time they open their mouth, it is to turn away wrath, it is to turn away rage, and it is to promote peace. The one who is not a peacemaker uses words to do exactly the opposite: to arouse anger, to stir up strife, to cause division, faction, and hatred in people through their words.

What words have you have spoken? Do they cause wrath for your wife or generate strife with your husband? Do they awaken anger in your children? Do they drive away, hurt, demean, or irritate people? Or are your words soft, sensible, docile, balanced, gracious, and able to promote peace?

Proverbs 26:20 also says, "Where no wood is, there the fire goeth out: so where there is no talebearer, the strife ceaseth." Slander stokes the fire of conflict, like the wood that keeps the fire going. However, the peacemaker knows the time to remain silent and to stop feeding discord, as James 1:19 teaches, "let every man be swift to hear, slow to speak, slow to wrath." He knows that by opening his mouth it will bring more strife, and, as he is not in that situation to promote discord, ends up closing his lips, only saying what is necessary—when it is necessary—because he knows that "in the multitude of words there wanteth not sin: but he that refraineth his lips is wise" (Prov 10:19).

In the face of these passages we can conclude that when the peacemaker uses words it is to turn away wrath. Also, when he is not using words it is not to feed dispute and division. How many have come to the conclusion that they should not have said something after thinking about it a little longer? The peacemaker is a person God has taught when to speak and when not to speak.

One of the marks that does not describe a peacemaker is that their tongue is similar to the "carpet of royalty." They always say a lot and much of what is said is not right. Their words hurt, demean, and displease.

Another thing that you will never see in a peacemaker is the morbid and refined taste for gossip. They cannot promote or agree with gossip, because it is one of the main instruments used to bring conflict. See Proverbs 11:13, "A talebearer [gossiper] revealeth secrets: but he that is of a faithful spirit concealeth the matter." Now, let's look at Leviticus 19:16, "Thou shalt not go up and down as a talebearer among thy people." These texts teach that the tale told, the gossip, brings dispute and division. Once the peacemaker begins to avoid conflict and turn from division, gossip is an abomination to him.

Note the strength of gossip in James 3:5–6, "Even so the tongue is a little member, and boasteth great things. Behold, how great a matter a little fire kindleth! And the tongue is a fire, a world of iniquity: so is the tongue among our members, that it defileth the whole body, and setteth on fire the course of nature; and it is set on fire of hell." James is stating that the tongue, when used to promote gossip, is able to ignite a forest. What does this mean? It is an instrument that can be used to instill strife, division, and hatred. Just as an uncontrolled fire can ruin a whole forest, a gossiper's tongue can destroy a great deal of property and lives!

Peacemakers do not open their mouths to spread rumors or gossip—they are not a "big-mouth," because gossip promotes strife rather than peace. Gossip promotes division and not union; gossip hardens the heart and does not soften it. Therefore, when a person gossips, that proves that the person is not a true Christian. For the one who keeps sowing discord among brothers and sisters, it is God's anger rather than his favor that rests on him (Prov 6:16–19). The peacemaker, the Christian, is exactly the opposite: they sow harmony in their home, among their brothers, among the leaders of the church and the members.

Fourth, we recognize peacemakers in their marriage. In search of the peacemaker, we must enter the living quarters of the home. Proverbs 21:9, 19 says, "It is better to dwell in a corner of the housetop, than with a brawling woman in a wide house.... It is better to dwell in the wilderness, than with a contentious and angry woman." Proverbs 27:15 reaffirms, "A continual dropping in a very rainy day and a contentious woman are alike."

Who is the contentious woman spoken of here? She is the irritated woman responsible for promoting strife. She annoys her husband, provokes him, and causes her husband to sin; she makes her husband tense and her children irritated. She is the woman who causes strife in the marriage, the one who does not promote peace in the home. Solomon states that it would be better to live in a deserted land than with a contentious woman, for in the wilderness there would be no strife promoted by the cranky woman.

We recognize the peacemaker in the marriage when one or both of the spouses work for the couple to be in harmony and peace. The biblical woman diffuses her husband's anger, reconciles herself with her husband, and does everything to promote peace between the couple. These are people who say, "I see my wife, she works hard for us to be at peace, she tries hard to diffuse my anger. She is a peacemaker."

A woman who was a biblical example of a peacemaker is portrayed in 1 Samuel 25:2–35. In this passage we see Abigail married to a man descending from Caleb called Nabal, who was very wealthy and had many properties, but was defiant, hard-hearted, and evil. Meanwhile Abigail's description in the passage was of a wise and beautiful woman.

One day David, who was fleeing from Saul, sent one of his soldiers to Nabal to inform him that the shearers of his sheep had been with David's army and they had been well treated. To help him out, David asked Nabal to send him the supplies he could. Nabal replied with mockery, saying, "Who is David? And who is the son of Jesse? I will give nothing to him." David's anger was aroused upon hearing such a disrespectful answer, and he decided he would kill that man and all of his family.

In the midst of this story, Abigail, the peacemaker, came on the scene. She made preparations to appease David's anger and promote peace. She sent supplies to him and went on her own to meet the angry warrior along the way. When she met David, Abigail fell at his feet, crying for mercy and confessing all the folly of her husband. She interceded so that David should spare them.

When he saw such a wise and humble interposition, David praised Abigail's actions and thanked her for being so prudent in stopping him from shedding blood through vengeance. That woman appeased David's wrath and promoted the peace between him and her husband Nabal.

Abigail was not alien to the sins and mistakes of her own husband, but she acted with prudence and fear, interceding for her husband, offering a peace offering for him and preventing him from being harmed by his own sin. What an example of the fear of God and peaceful fidelity in marriage! Dear wife, are you like that in your marriage?

Let us now look at an example of a woman who was not a peacemaker. She appears in Job 2:9–10, "Then said his wife unto him, Dost thou still retain thine integrity? Curse God, and die. But he said unto her, Thou speakest as one of the foolish women speaketh. What? Shall we receive good at the hand of God, and shall we not receive evil? In all this did not Job sin with his lips." The context of this passage is related to Job's pain, who inexplicably had lost ten children, all of his properties, all of his cattle, and all his servants. Finally, Job had also lost his health, being wounded from horrible skin sores right up to the top of his head.

His wife saw his state of complete disaster and acute prostration. As if that wasn't enough, she came to him with her foolish counsel, suggesting that he should say his last words against God and die! She provoked Job's anger and irritated him. With her attitude, she increased Job's pain even more. Instead of Job's wife consoling him in all the confusion that had fallen upon him, she tried to put her husband against God!

Dear reader, do not act like Nabal, in a belligerent manner. Neither act as Job's wife, foolishly! Do not lead your spouse to sin against God. Understand their pain, respect their moment of weakness. Do not divide your home, but relieve their pain, carry their burden and try to promote the reconciliation.

Fifth, we recognize a peacemaker in their family by the way they treat their children. See what Ephesians 6:4 says, "And, ye fathers [and mothers], provoke not your children to wrath: but bring them up in the nurture and admonition of the Lord." The peacemaking parent does not provoke the child's anger, irritating the child, humiliating the child, exposing the child, and injuring the child. The peacemaker promotes harmony between him and his child.

There are parents who drive their children kilometers away from them each week, because they provoke them to anger, generating strife, division, conflict, and a real war between them. This is not the role of the peacemaker. The role of peacemakers is to kiss their children and give them a hug, to hear, pray with, and cry for their children. They are patient, benign, and kind, always looking out for the good of their children. They exercise their parental authority, but always with love.

Colossians 3:21 says, "Fathers, provoke not your children to anger, lest they be discouraged." Do you think the peacemaker takes away someone's good cheer? The peacemaker promotes good cheer and encourages the child. The one who is not a peacemaker discourages their children, demeans them, and slanders them, making them feel completely useless and worthless. Dear reader, are you a friend of your child? Is your daughter your friend, mother? Are they happy to be with you?

Sixth, we recognize peacemakers because they are preachers of the gospel. We must remember that the task of the peacemaker is to promote peace between enemy parties. Every sinner is the enemy of God, and the "wrath of God is revealed from heaven against all ungodliness and unrighteousness of men" (Rom 1:18). Yes, there is a barrier between God and the sinner, a conflict between the two. What is the role of the peacemaker? To proclaim the gospel to the sinner, so that he may be reconciled with God!

Romans 10:15 says, "And how shall they preach, except they be sent? As it is written, How beautiful are the feet of them that preach the gospel of peace, and bring glad tidings of good things." The Bible calls the gospel, "the gospel of peace," because it reconciles men with God. Second Corinthians 5:20 affirms, "Now then we are ambassadors for Christ, as though God did beseech you by us. We pray you in Christ's stead, be ye reconciled to God."

Who is the ambassador of whom Paul speaks? It is the peacemaker! It is he who preaches to sinners to be reconciled with God, who calls sinners to repentance, leading them

to the faith. How? He does this by proclaiming the gospel, and when he preaches the gospel, he promotes peace between God and the sinner.

The peacemaker is an evangelist who always seeks to lead people to the faith through the proclamation of the gospel, calling men to repentance. Peacemakers preach the Scriptures, for they know that this is the only way to promote restoration with God (Rom 10:17).

When peacemakers see the escalation of sin in society and the nations at war, their hearts hurt, because they know that those people are fighting with God, needing to be reconciled with him through the gospel of Jesus Christ.

Finally, before we talk about the reward of the peacemaker, it must be said that it is an honor for a man or woman to be recognized as a peacemaker. Proverbs 20:3 makes the following observation, "It is an honor for a man to cease from strife: but every fool will be meddling." The peacemaker is exactly that kind of man or woman. He or she always seeks to hoist the white flag of peace. Treating their neighbor well is not optional for the peacemaker, but a duty he follows closely.

The peacemaker is continually watching to ensure that their state of honor, of peace with God and peace with men, is not tarnished. They are the ones who watch their mouth so that no filthy word comes from it, but only one that edifies its hearers (Eph 4:29).

Promised Reward for the Peacemaker

Finally, what is the promise for the peacemaker? "They shall be called children of God" (Matt 5:9). This is one of the most beautiful promises in the Bible. The peacemakers will be recognized as children of God.

First, they will be recognized as God's children by God himself, as Romans 8:16 says, "The Spirit itself beareth witness with our spirit, that we are the children of God." Those who enjoy inner peace even in trials; those who work, pray, fast, and weep to keep peace in the home; those who speak with sweetness and always seek the benefit of God and neighbor: where you see a Christian like this, know that they were adopted by God, recognized by him as a legitimate child.

In addition to being recognized by God as their children, peacemakers are seen as such by the people around them. Ask a peacemaker's wife who he is at home. Ask his children. Ask his colleagues at work or school. The people around them recognize them as peacemakers, because someone with this character given from God does not go unnoticed in a world full of conflict and strife.

Therefore, the peacemakers will be recognized by God himself and by society as true Christians who have a genuine faith, attested by works.

Conclusion

Dear reader, I want to close with a word of encouragement. You may not be the peacemaker, or even close to it. There is a powerful God in heaven, attentive to the prayers of men, who can transform your state, reconciling you with him; he is the one from whom reconciliation will flow through you to others.

Don't waste any more time; don't hurt anyone else. Go to God, who can do everything!

CHAPTER 10

Blessed Are the Persecuted

After studying seven beatitudes, we come to the eighth and last of this series of identifiable traits that the Lord Jesus presents of the true Christian.

As previously stated, we are faced with the greatest sermon of all time, proclaimed by the greatest preacher of all time, who handed over the greatest constitution of a kingdom never before known. With this speech, Jesus revealed the character of the genuine servant of the blessed kingdom of heaven.

The last beatitude brings the teaching that every child of God will be persecuted. Jesus states in Matthew 5:10–12, "Blessed are they which are persecuted for righteousness' sake: for theirs is the kingdom of heaven. Blessed are ye, when men shall revile you, and persecute you, and shall say all manner of evil against you falsely, for my sake. Rejoice, and be exceeding glad: for great is your reward in heaven: for so persecuted they the prophets which were before you."

While the other seven beatitudes describe essential traits of the Christian's character, the final beatitude delivers the consequences for possessing all of the aforementioned traits. How does the world receive and react to the genuine Christian who portrays the Beatitudes? Jesus said the world reacts with persecution and hostility.

You might think the world like meek, humble, broken, and sincere people. Would these people not be well looked upon, worthy of praise, applause, and love? Would they not be esteemed for having such qualities? No. Jesus said they would not; he said that the meek, the humble, the poor, and the broken would not be loved, esteemed, or praised, but rather would be relentlessly persecuted. This is the reaction of the world to the holy and distinct people of God: hostility. The term persecution describes the oppression, harassment, rejection, and hatred faced by the true Christian.

Therefore, dear reader, the last beatitude authenticates your Christianity. How do you know you have the other Beatitudes? If the eighth—being persecuted for the sake of righteousness and love for Christ—is a reality in your life. Persecution is the standard for a genuine, authentic Christian. It is normal for them to suffer slander, for lies to be spoken against them, plans being forged against them, and power games planned to bring them harm. All of this is normal and must be expected in the life of a Christian. If you study early church history (especially the first four centuries), you'll find the "holy martyrs," those brothers and sisters who died eaten by beasts in the Roman Coliseum, who were crucified or burned alive, or who were drowned or pierced by spears and swords—all for testifying of their faith in Christ.

However, they did not die with the recognition of heroes of a noble cause, as servants of God, or as saints. They were persecuted for being cannibals, for they claimed that they ate the body and drank the blood of Christ. They were accused of orgies and incest because they gathered as a body of brothers and sisters in Christ, so their opponents thought that they committed immoralities among members of their own blood family. They were accused of atheism, because they worshiped a God who they could not show through images or symbols, so they were considered worshipers of a nonexistent divinity. They died as heretics, witches, prostitutes, and bandits.

If a widespread persecution comes in our age—and who can say that with the nature of our world today this will not come to pass—you will not be persecuted as a man or woman of God; you will be persecuted as someone who supposedly committed the greatest of atrocities. You will be considered an enemy of the human race. Your love for God and your sanctification will mean nothing to the world, and all sorts of lies, blasphemies, injustices, and evil may be attributed to you.

The Reality and Cause of Persecution

So then, to deal with this solemn matter, we will divide this subject into two parts: "the reality of persecution" and "the cause of persecution."

When I write "the reality of persecution," I mean it will be real, and it will happen. Things in the West have changed dramatically in recent decades. Previously, we had in this part of the world the solid defense of Christian values, which included valuing the family, civil obedience, and a great respect for religion. We have seen the rise of a new time, in which civil unions have been encouraged, and corruption abounds on this side of the world; indifference to the old education that taught the values of the Christian worldview has been quickly replaced by an atheistic, hedonistic mentality.

Together with this, we have seen the astonishing Muslim advances into that which was formerly the stronghold of the Christian faith, the West. We have already lost count of how many Islamic-related terrorist attacks have occurred in the world following the attack on the World Trade Center in New York, USA, on September 11, 2001. We cannot be deceived; it is part of the Muslim religion, taught by Mohammed, that all heretics, that is, those who do not convert to the Islamic faith, must be killed. There is no, what many call, "moderate Islamism," because it is Allah's express command that war against all non-Muslims—and us, Christians—is something that receives divine favor and reward.

We are rapidly approaching the words of Jesus, "yea, the time cometh, that whosoever killeth you will think that he doeth God service" (Jn 16:2). As well as persecuting us, the enemy will kill us while thinking they are doing good. You need to know: there will be persecution against your life. It is impossible for this not to happen; it is impossible for a faithful believer not to suffer persecution. You will be harassed, hated, rejected, and doors will close to you because of your faith. Throughout the history of the Christian church, Christians have paid a high price for their faith.

However, Matthew 5:10 says, "Blessed are the persecuted." Observing the original Greek tense of this passage, we could read it in English as: "blessed are those who have been and are being persecuted." Jesus said in this passage that the Christian, while on earth, will be persecuted, and will suffer hostility, rejection, and hatred. Looking at the Old and New Testaments, we can see that God's chosen people never had complete peace in this world. Jesus, speaking about this said, "for so persecuted they the prophets which were before you" (Matt 5:12).

We could list several Old Testament prophets who suffered persecution; even David was relentlessly persecuted by Saul. If you read the Psalms, and the books of Samuel and the Chronicles, you will see this holy one of God being unfairly oppressed. In the vast majority of the psalms that David wrote, he spoke of "how the number of my enemies has increased. . . . they are more than the hair of my head."

Elijah, the great prophet, was persecuted by Jezebel and Ahab, the wicked king and queen of Israel. After the prophet ascended on Mount Carmel, calling the people to repentance and proving the truth of Yahweh with wonderful signs, massacring Baal's prophets, and praying that the rain would return, Jezebel threatened to kill him, swearing that she would end his life! Elijah was not a beloved prophet, nor was he nice. He was repudiated by the king of Israel, hunted by the queen of Israel, persecuted, and sworn to death.

What about Isaiah, the Messianic prophet? Isaiah was persecuted to the point where history narrates—possibly in the reign of Manasseh—that he was sawn in two (see Heb 11:37). Imagine the cruelty employed in the death of this saint of God.

Jeremiah, the weeping prophet, so loved his people that he prophesied severely against them, so he didn't have to see their destruction! He was persecuted by the wicked king Zedekiah, imprisoned in a well, and was tortured, forgotten, and discredited. Jeremiah's ministry—one of the greatest saints this world has ever seen—was marked by hostility and rejection.

One anonymous author said of Jeremiah: "Never has it been imposed on a mortal man a more crushing burden than that placed upon Jeremiah. Throughout the history of the Jewish race there has never been such an example of intensity, sincerity, unrelieved suffering, fearless proclamation of the message of God, tireless intercession of a prophet for his people, as can be seen in Jeremiah's ministry. But, the tragedy of his life was this: he preached to deaf ears, and received hatred only in exchange for his love for his fellow citizens."

Who doesn't remember the persecutions of Daniel, the man that God loved dearly? He was thrown into the lions' den, just because he prayed three times a day to his God! The death sentence that he was given was for the worst criminals in the empire, and it would have ensured that his enemies were comforted by knowing he was torn apart and eaten, suffering a slow painful death for his faithfulness to the Lord. If God hadn't delivered him, it would certainly have been his end.

When we come to the New Testament, we find even greater suffering. Paul described the state of the apostles in 1 Corinthians 4:9–13:

> For I think that God hath set forth us the apostles last, as it were appointed to death: for we are made a spectacle unto the world, and to angels, and to men. We are fools for Christ's sake, but ye are wise in Christ; we are weak, but ye are strong; ye are honorable, but we are despised. Even unto this present hour we both hunger, and thirst, and are naked, and are buffeted, and have no certain dwelling place; And labor, working with our own hands. Being reviled, we bless; being persecuted, we suffer it: Being defamed, we intreat: we are made as the filth of the world, and are the offscouring of all things unto this day.

Look at the character of God's holy ministers of the past! Tell me: do you think the above description fits the "apostles" of today? We hear of many so-called "apostles" in the present evangelical world, and do you think they have a third of what the Apostle Paul declared? These people are false apostles, devout wolves, and liars. They live in luxurious comfort and boost their own egos. They are not suffering, and they are not persecuted. The only discomfort they have is to continue with their lies to keep their masses of followers deceived, because they could be spending that time enjoying even more of the delicacies of this world.

Jesus Christ, the founder of our faith, the edifier of the church, was the first to be persecuted in the new covenant. He was discredited, resisted, rejected, mocked, arrested, tortured, and killed. Then came his apostles: they all died as martyrs, except for John. They died without anything, forgotten and abandoned, lacking the most basic things.

In the year 60 A.D. there was the first great persecution of Christians under the Roman Emperor Nero (37–68). The Christians were killed, tortured, burned alive, thrown to the lions, arrested, and had their property confiscated. Do you know what their crime was? Believing in Jesus! It was for believing in Jesus that they were harassed, because they were holy. And their persecution did not cease with the death of Nero, but continued under the emperors Domitian (51–96), Trajan (53–117), Alexander (208–235), Diocletian (244–311) and so many others.

When we get to the church of the Middle Ages, from the twelfth century inquisition onwards, we come to a period of great Christian persecution, especially of those who did not subject themselves to the orders and counter-orders of the papacy. They were burned, drowned, and hanged, suffering unimaginable torture. What about the women of that time? When they did not heed to the sexual desires of wicked Roman Catholic priests, they were accused of witchcraft, abused, and were then killed with the refined methods of cruelty!

In the city of Prague, which was located in Bohemia, the pre-Reformer Jan Hus (1369–1415), influenced by the ideas of another English reformer, John Wycliffe (1320–1384), was persecuted, arrested and martyred by fire. What was his crime? To argue that everyone should exercise the free examination of the Scriptures, being able to read God's Word in their own national language.

Then we have William Tyndale (1494–1536), who is considered by many the first Puritan. He was severely hunted by agents of the English King Henry VIII (1491–1547), because he translated the Scriptures into English; he was eventually captured by ambush in Belgium and burned alive.

When Mary Tudor (1516–1558) came to power, after the short reign of her brother Edward VI (1537–1553), intense persecution of the Puritans was unleashed, which caused the death of hundreds of Protestant Christians. The cruelty and complete lack of mercy of this queen gave her the title of "Bloody Mary."

Notice that all these people were killed not because they had committed adultery or because they were thieves or swindlers; they were not persecuted because they had lied or fornicated. They were persecuted because of their faith, their righteous living, and for being servants of God. Someone once said, "believers will always be persecuted as long as they live in this world."

John 15:18–20 says, "If the world hate you, ye know that it hated me before it hated you. If ye were of the world, the world would love his own: but because ye are not of the world, but I have chosen you out of the world, therefore the world hateth you. Remember the word that I said unto you, the servant is not greater than his lord. If they have persecuted me, they will also persecute you; if they have kept my saying, they will keep yours also."

It is as if Jesus had said, "If the world loved me, I would be from the world; if I had the sympathy of the world, I would be from the world; if I had the praise and status of the world, I would be from the world. But, as I am not of the world, the world hates and persecutes me." He then adds to that by saying that as they persecuted him for not being of the world, they would also persecute his disciples because they were not of the world.

Matthew 10:21–23 states, "And the brother shall deliver up the brother to death, and the father the child: and the children shall rise up against their parents, and cause them to be put to death. And ye shall be hated of all men for my name's sake: but he that endureth to the end shall be saved. But when they persecute you in this city, flee ye into another: for verily I say unto you, Ye shall not have gone over the cities of Israel, till the Son of man be come." Why are Christians hated? Because of His Name! Christians will be hated for looking like Christ, and for the Spirit's work of sanctification in their lives, exhibing meekness, humility, and mercy.

However, what have we seen today? It is "fashionable" for Christians to be well with the world, walking hand in hand with it and making alliances with its standards! There is a certain doctrine which teaches that we must be well and at peace with everyone. That is not true, because by acting in this way, the absolute values of the gospel would be negotiated and the price of friendship with the world would be disobedience to God. Many are trying to gather together that which God has separated! See what Luke 6:26 says, "Woe unto you, when all men shall speak well of you! For so did their fathers to the false prophets."

If everything the wicked says about you is praise, honor, and camaraderie, there is something wrong with your conduct! If they are your best friends and partners, there is something terribly wrong with your life, for Jesus said "woe" unto you, that is, you are cursed when all who hate God love you!

2 Timothy 3:12 attests, "Yea, and all that will live godly in Christ Jesus shall suffer persecution." This verse is in a pastoral letter from the Apostle Paul to Timothy. As a senior pastor, Paul was warning the young minister Timothy that he would have much opposition in his Christian ministry. If you wish to be holy, to be a man or woman of God, a scholar of Scripture, a man or woman of prayer: prepare yourself. You will suffer persecution. The more holy you are, the more persecuted you will be. The more you pray, the more demons will oppress you. The more you fast, the more you will be hated. The more compassionate you are, the more opposition you will face. Look at Jesus in the same situation, "Jesus answered them, many good works have I shewed you from my Father; for which of those works do ye stone me?" (Jn 10:32).

Acts 14:22 reads, "Confirming the souls of the disciples, and exhorting them to continue in the faith, and that we must through much tribulation enter into the kingdom of God." Paul gave this exhortation to the brothers of Lystra, Iconium, and Antioch who were being molested shortly after his conversion and during the first stages of his new faith. He consoled them and told them not to be scared, for persecution would be normal. For us, we have the same recommendation: we will be persecuted. The hostility of the world that hates the Lord is real against the children of God.

Now that we know that persecution is real, let's examine the cause of it. Jesus said, "Blessed are they which are persecuted for righteousness' sake" (Matt 5:10). It is important to clarify that not all of the persecuted are blessed. There are many who are persecuted around the world for various reasons, but they are not blessed. We must understand that the blessed is the one who suffers persecution because of the righteousness of God, for their genuine faith in the gospel.

So what does it not mean to be persecuted for righteousness? It is not suffering merely for opposing dictatorial regimes, seeking fairer working conditions, or fighting for noble social ideals. It is not a question of the political persecution of those who are against a government. It is not a woman harassed because she is fighting for the right of other women to have an active voice in a certain area. Jesus did not address this type of persecution—which is also unjust in many cases. Also people who are being persecuted are not

blessed because they are good people or because they are misunderstood by others. The text is not addressing these sorts of trials and sufferings.

Jesus is also not addressing any kind of persecution that a church may suffer for negligence. There are many contexts in which a church may be suffering opposition due to unfair causes. For example, suppose the sound system of a congregation is an affront to the limits set by law, causing constant discomfort in the neighborhood. If the church is sued, it cannot say that "the wicked are trying to stop God's cause." What is happening is disrespect for the law and to the well-being of the community around that church. It is a bad testimony of the church to the wicked, and not persecution.

The persecution that is "blessed" is that which is for the sake of righteousness. In other words, blessed are those who are persecuted for being like Jesus and following him in their lives. Those persecuted for righteousness are those persecuted for weeping, for being meek, for having a desire for holiness, for being merciful, for being clean of heart, and for being peacemakers!

Matthew 5:13–16 says, "Ye are the salt of the earth: but if the salt have lost his savor, wherewith shall it be salted? It is thenceforth good for nothing, but to be cast out, and to be trodden under foot of men. Ye are the light of the world. A city that is set on an hill cannot be hid: neither do men light a candle, and put it under a bushel, but on a candlestick; and it giveth light unto all that are in the house. Let your light so shine before men, that they may see your good works, and glorify your Father which is in heaven."

Christians are hated because they are salt and light. They have the characteristics of the light, which are the Beatitudes. Their good works, which imitate those of the Lord Jesus, are so pure and so contrary to the corrupt standard of this world that there is no other choice for the wicked than to hate them and to do everything to exterminate them. Why? Because as long as they are close, their light will illuminate all the evil of those who do not live like them!

See another text that confirms this truth, "And this is the condemnation, that light is come into the world, and men loved darkness rather than light, because their deeds were evil. For every one that doeth evil hateth the light, neither cometh to the light, lest his deeds should be reproved" (Jn 3:19–20). The world hates light—and all Christians who are of the light— because light denounces darkness. This is why the world hates us: our conduct exposes them, manifesting their wickedness and sin.

Another reason why the world hates Christians is because of their absolute values. John 14:6 says, "Jesus saith unto him, I am the way, the truth, and the life: no man cometh unto the Father, but by me." Did you see how Jesus constructed the phrase? He used the definite article "the." He did not use the indefinite article "a." One of the reasons the church is hated is that it expresses its assertions with the definite article. The truth is not "a" truth, "an" option, or "a" possibility. No, it is the truth, it is the absolute option and the only possibility, which means there are no concessions. The church says that either we follow the exclusive, absolute truth of God, or we will never reach God.

In a pluralistic and relativistic world, everyone who affirms the definite way—the absolute truth—and the righteous life instead of the other various ways and possibilities will be harassed. The world will never be bothered with those who follow Christ and another faith; the gospel and lies; the Christian faith and sensuality; the Word of God and Buddha's teachings. The world will hate those who assert themselves as followers "just and only" of the Lamb. They cannot tolerate this because they are a threat to their system.

Here, dear reader, you are put before a test without escape: is the world your enemy or your friend? Does it resist you or love you? Does your commitment to the Lord Jesus deal a mortal blow against all other forms of plural religiosity or support them? You will be tested for being fully committed to Christ!

Forms of Persecution Found in Scripture

Let us now talk about the form of persecution. How will it come? How does it show itself in the lives of true Christians?

In order not to be errant, we need to know that there are various forms of persecution. Not everyone will be martyred, not everyone will have their property confiscated, their homes burned down, or suffer an attack on their life. There are various forms and levels of persecution that a Christian can suffer. The only sure fact is that everyone, without exception, will be persecuted in some way. Below, we will see three ways that persecution can take place against a faithful follower of Jesus.

Social Attacks

Matthew 5:11 says, "Blessed are ye, when men shall revile you, and persecute you." The Greek word for one of the forms of persecution called libel is oneidezo, which means insulting with reproach, shaming, humiliating, and mistreating. It points to social persecution. You will be mistreated by the ungodly society. There will be oppression, rejection, and humiliation at school, at work, or within the family itself. You may have your salary compromised, a promotion denied, or your family relationships shaken simply for being a Christian. They will mock you, shame you because of your faith, reject you and exclude you from the possibilities that for others are normal. You may be ignored; Jesus said in Luke 6:22, "Blessed are ye, when men shall hate you, and when they shall separate you from their company, and shall reproach you, and cast out your name as evil, for the Son of Man's sake." This text speaks of social isolation. The world will see you as a "plague," a "pest," and no one will want to stay close to you; there will be social rejection because of your faith. Your friends will end their friendships, and they will not call you anymore. They will not invite you any more to parties or celebrations, for they do not share your faith. Because you do not covet your neighbor's wife, do not rejoice in lies, do not delight in worldly music, and do not condone drunkenness, you will be a hindrance, a stumbling block. No one will want your company, because you will disturb their sinful entertainment. You will be considered a "spoilsport."

Keep in mind that the Christian standard is established in Psalm 1:1, "Blessed is the man that walketh not in the counsel of the ungodly, nor standeth in the way of sinners, nor sitteth in the seat of the scornful." Therefore, for not approving the conduct of the wicked, you will be rejected and suffer social persecution. If this has never happened to you or has ceased to occur, examine your life and repent before God.

Verbal Attacks

Jesus also says in Matthew 5:11, "and shall say all manner of evil against you." The word lying in Greek is pseudomai, from which the English prefix "pseudo" is derived, which means false. The Christian will be attacked through lies and falsehoods against their faith, their life, and their conduct. You will be slandered and falsely discussed. The word "evil" comes from the Greek poneros which means something guilty, degenerated, malicious, and perverse.

Therefore, the Christian will be attacked with lies that will impute upon them false and dishonest facts, blaming them of vile, malicious, and perverse things. You will not be persecuted as an honest person; you will be accused of practicing false crimes, acts of immorality, adultery, and fraud. You will be counted among thieves and scoundrels. They will call you a hypocrite and affirm that you are of bad character.

In the early church, Christians were often accused of incest, because their enemies claimed that they had heard them call their wives "sisters." They called them sisters not because they were of the same blood, but because of the bond of brotherly love through Christ that leads us to call Christians brothers and sisters! If this has occurred in the past and in various other times in church history, it is true that it continues to occur today and will still occur against the people of God.

Jesus said that they will say "all manner of evil against you." The enemies will use every possible kind of lying attacks against the true Christian, with the purpose of bringing them down, embarrassing them, staining their reputation, extorting money, obtaining their silence, and persuading them to abandon the faith.

This is how they persecuted John the Baptist as we read in Matthew 11:18, "For John came neither eating nor drinking, and they say, he hath a devil!" Who did they say had a demon? John the Baptist, the greatest of those born of a woman (Matt 11:11), the one who was filled with the Holy Spirit from the womb (Luke 1:15, 41), who was called by the prophet Isaiah as "the voice of him that crieth in the desert" and prepared the way of the Messiah (Isa 40:3). They persecuted John the Baptist saying that his ministry was the work of demons!

Furthermore, Jesus too was attacked verbally: "Now the chief priests, and elders, and all the council, sought false witness against Jesus, to put him to death. But found none: yea, though many false witnesses came" (Matt 26:59–60). Who was Jesus? The God-man, Lord of lords and King of kings, the most blessed of the whole universe! He, sinless and completely clean, was falsely accused by those who wanted to condemn him unjustly. They called him blasphemous and a liar (see Matt 9:2–3), as if he had said lies against God!

They accused him of being a child of prostitution (gr. porneia), because they believed that he had been born of illicit sexual relations of his mother, calling him a bastard and illegitimate son (see Jn 8:41–48). The evil Pharisees went after the history of Jesus's conception, remembering that Mary had become pregnant while she was a virgin, and that Joseph had tried to leave her because he thought that Mary had betrayed him (Matt 1:18–25). They argued that if Jesus had not been born of the union of Joseph and Mary, then he was a bastard! Think about it: the enemies have gone back more than thirty years in time to accuse someone who was perfectly righteous and the Son of God himself who begot him in Mary's womb by the Holy Spirit! I would like you to realize, reader, that there is no limit to the evil men will use to attack a righteous man.

Physical Attacks

Third, Christians will suffer physical attacks of persecution. Matthew 5:11 speaks too of this form of persecution: "Blessed are ye, when men shall . . . persecute you . . . for my sake." The Greek term for persecution is dioko, which means running quickly, for the purpose of capturing someone or something. Jesus was saying that there would be such severe persecutions that the evil ones would run after the disciples to capture them, and they would need to flee or they would not be able to preserve their own lives.

Second Corinthians 11:24–25 speaks of a situation in which Paul physically suffered persecution for righteousness's sake: "Of the Jews five times received I forty stripes save one. Thrice was I beaten with rods, once was I stoned, thrice I suffered shipwreck, a night and a day I have been in the deep." It seems like an unbelievable story, but Paul suffered all these attacks against his physical integrity, against his life—all of this because of his faith in Christ Jesus.

Acts 7:59–60 states, "And they stoned Stephen, calling upon God, and saying, Lord Jesus, receive my spirit! And he kneeled down, and cried with a loud voice: Lord, lay not this sin to their charge! With these words, he fell asleep." The physical persecution against Stephen was so strong that he died. In his life, just as it can be in ours, the Scripture was fulfilled where it says, "As it is written, for thy sake we are killed all the day long; we are accounted as sheep for the slaughter" (Rom 8:36).

Matthew 27:27–31 reads, "Then the soldiers of the governor took Jesus into the common hall, and gathered unto him the whole band of soldiers. And they stripped him, and put on him a scarlet robe; And when they had platted a crown of thorns, they put it upon his head, and a reed in his right hand: and they bowed the knee before him, and mocked him, saying, hail, King of the Jews! And they spit upon him, and took the reed, and smote him on the head. And after that they had mocked him, they took the robe off from him, and put his own raiment on him. And led him away to crucify him."

Persecution against Jesus came in all three forms as narrated in this passage. He suffered a physical attack, slander, and social rejection. There was the Ruler of the universe—the One who brought all things into existence and supported it with his Word—alone and abandoned by all (social rejection). The Roman soldiers spat on him, mocked him, and humiliated him (verbal attack). Those same soldiers beat his head, whipped him, and took him to be killed by crucifixion (physical attack).

What a warning these passages give us, teaching that we should be prepared to suffer as the saints who came before us and the Lord Jesus himself suffered for the sake of righteousness. Not all will suffer in the same way or with the same intensity, but we must know that our God has warned us that, because we are his disciples, persecution and hostility will come.

The Persecutors

By whom will we be persecuted? Who will be the antagonists of the true Christian and of the church of the living God? First of all, as we have seen above, the Christian will be persecuted by the fallen world and its anti-God system. See John 17:14–16, "I have given them thy word; and the world hath hated them, because they are not of the world, even as I am not of the world. I pray not that thou shouldest take them out of the world, but that thou shouldest keep them from the evil. They are not of the world, even as I am not of the world."

Secondly, the Christian will be persecuted by false Christians. It may be that man or woman sitting next to you at church or those who are "nominal Christians." By whom was Jesus most persecuted? By false Jews, those who went to the synagogue and to the temple, who prayed to Yahweh; they were the ones who harassed and killed Jesus, the Messiah of Israel himself. See John 10:29–32, "My Father, which gave them me, is greater than all; and no man is able to pluck them out of my Father's hand. I and my Father are one. Then the Jews took up stones again to stone him. Jesus answered them, Many good works have I shewed you from my Father; for which of those works do ye stone me?"

Who were the main persecutors of the Apostle Paul? The Jews, the false Christians, the wolves in sheep's clothing in the midst of God's people. It was they who oppressed the apostle the most, as we see in Acts 13:43–50:

> Now when the congregation was broken up, many of the Jews and religious proselytes followed Paul and Barnabas: who, speaking to them, persuaded them to continue in the grace of God. Paul and Barnabas go to the Gentiles. And the next Sabbath day came almost the whole city together to hear the word of God. But when the Jews saw the multitudes, they were filled with envy, and spake against those things which were spoken by Paul, contradicting and blaspheming. Then Paul and Barnabas waxed bold, and said, it was necessary that the word of God should first have been spoken to you: but seeing ye put it from you, and judge yourselves unworthy of everlasting life, lo, we turn to the Gentiles. For so hath the Lord commanded us, saying, I have set thee to be a light of the Gentiles,

that thou shouldest be for salvation unto the ends of the earth. And when the Gentiles heard this, they were glad, and glorified the word of the Lord: and as many as were ordained to eternal life believed. And the word of the Lord was published throughout all the region. But the Jews stirred up the devout and honorable women, and the chief men of the city, and raised persecution against Paul and Barnabas, and expelled them out of their coasts.

When persecution of the people of God is carried out by false Christians, they do worse things than the ungodly. They lie, bribe, corrupt, sell, and falsify; they are the ones to make the phone calls, send messages, and finally they do everything they can for the sole purpose of bringing the faithful down. Their pleasure is to ruin the true Christian, to make them bleed and be completely humiliated before everyone.

Never forget that the mark of a true Christian is to love the other brothers and sisters, while false Christians, the goats, have their pleasure in the fall and humiliation of the servants of the Lord.

Thirdly, the Christian will be persecuted by the family. Matthew 10:34–36 says, "Think not that I am come to send peace on earth: I came not to send peace, but a sword. For I am come to set a man at variance against his father, and the daughter against her mother, and the daughter in law against her mother in law. And a man's foes shall be they of his own household."

Prepare to suffer persecution at home, in the midst of your own family. If you have a wicked family, they are in darkness. When the Lord saves you, you become light in that place; soon everyone will oppose you. A wife may get along well with her husband, but when she is converted, she suffers opposition from her husband. The children live in accord with the parents, but when they are converted, the parents begin to persecute them. How many cases have we heard of husbands who abandon and divorce the wife when she is converted or from cases where the woman abandons and divorces her husband when he is converted?

We must be aware that persecution can reach our family. We will be persecuted by the relatives. There will be discomfort, hostility, and rejection in the home. Even when there are nominal Christians in the family, and another member of the house is genuinely regenerated, he who is a new creature will suffer with false believers within his own family! Think: people who listen to the same preaching, sing the same hymns, gather in the same church, and live in the same house will oppose the true Christians, who have the Beatitudes engraved upon their lives.

The Response and the Reward of the Persecuted

What should our reaction be in the face of persecution? The text of the Sermon on the Mount says, "Rejoice, and be exceeding glad" (Matt 5:12). How should we act in the face of persecution? There must be joy! Jesus does not want it to be the opposite: murmuring, slandering, anguish, and sadness. At the same time, Jesus is not saying that the Christian is masochistic, finding deep pleasure in his own suffering, who laughs when taking a beating. That's not it. We are sad, but by divine grace, we do not let despair and depression take hold of us. See the teaching of James 1:2 and Philippians 2:17–18, "My brethren, count it all joy when ye fall into divers temptations"; "Yea, and if I be offered upon the sacrifice and service of your faith, I joy, and [rejoice] with you all. For the same cause also do ye joy, and [rejoice] with me." These biblical texts invite us to rejoice when we are persecuted because of our love and service to the Lord!

This was what happened to Peter and John, "When they had called the apostles, and beaten them, they commanded that they should not speak in the name of Jesus, and let them go. And they departed from the presence of the council, rejoicing that they were counted worthy to suffer shame for his Name" (Acts 5:40–41).

First Peter 4:12–14 shows that Christians can be joyful during suffering is because they suffer in the likeness of Christ, knowing that they will be rewarded when the blessed Lord returns to fetch them; see, "Beloved, think it not strange concerning the fiery trial which is to try you, as though some strange thing happened unto you. but rejoice, inasmuch as ye are partakers of Christ's sufferings; that, when his glory shall be revealed, ye may be glad also with exceeding joy. If ye be reproached for the name of Christ, happy are ye; for the spirit of glory and of God resteth upon you." What is the reward for the blessed, who will suffer every kind and intensity of persecution for the sake of righteousness? Matthew 5:12 replies, "Rejoice, and be exceeding glad: for great is your reward in heaven: for so persecuted they the prophets which were before you."

The first reward while living on earth is to be compared to the prophets. This authenticates our conversion and assures us that we are beloved children of God. It is as if he himself had said, "Do you remember Jeremiah, Isaiah, Haggai, John the Baptist, and Micah? If you suffer persecution because of my righteousness, you are resembling them, you are replacing them, showing that you are God's servants as much as they were in their days."

This is deep evidence that someone is saved, that they have been redeemed, they have inherited eternal life, and are true Christians. This confirmation brings joy! This path that many brothers and sisters in Christ have walked before us leads to the same end: joy! So let us rejoice!

The second reward says that the true Christian will have a gift for suffering. Every trial, every temptation borne, burden carried, slander heard—all of this for the love of the Son of God will be rewarded. The reward will be great, presented in a glorious way. Where will the true

Christian receive this reward? In heaven, just as the verse says. The eternal reward of the saints will not be in this life. Here on earth, you will lose and win, you will get some things right and some things wrong, you will laugh and you will cry. However, when you enter through those gates of splendor—where the unclean will not enter and sin will no longer exist—there, in the blessed eternal home, you will hear him say, "Come, ye blessed of my Father! Inherit the kingdom prepared for you from the foundation of the world" (Matt 25:34).

Our eternal dwelling, our city is not of this world, as it says in Hebrews 13:13–14, "Let us go forth therefore unto him without the camp, bearing his reproach. For here have we no continuing city, but we seek one to come." Dear reader, this is the greatness of the gospel, this is the greatness of Christianity: to be persecuted for loving Christ is to be blessed here, and it will be our crown of faith in heaven, where we will reap a great reward.

Conclusion

Blessed are you who suffer persecution, because it is proof that your life has passed the test of the Beatitudes. You have all seven Beatitudes, which testify that you are a true Christian. No one can steal the inheritance that awaits you in heaven with glory! Wait, your crown of righteousness is coming, and soon the Lord Jesus will give it to you with great joy.

CONCLUSION

A Word to the Blessed

I started this book by talking about salt, and I will close it in the same way. You who have followed the study of the Beatitudes so far may realize that Jesus closed this beautiful discourse in Matthew 5:12.

However, soon after that, in verse 13, Christ made a statement about the Christian, saying, "You are the salt of the earth." What did he mean by this statement and why was it pronounced immediately after the Beatitudes? In the previous verses, Jesus had described the character of the true Christian, listing his peculiar characteristics, and in verse 13 he exposed the reason or the purpose of someone having the Beatitudes.

The salt has at least two great qualities. The first of these is related to giving flavor to the food. This is not difficult to understand, since if you have already eaten some food without the presence of salt (especially food that was unpleasant to eat), you might realize that without that salt the flavor is lacking or there is no taste at all.

When Jesus proclaimed that true Christians are the salt of the earth, he was saying that just as salt gives flavor to the food in which it is placed, in the same way the genuine children of God must season or give flavor to this world. That is, men, after they have been truly converted, must influence this world when they come into contact with it. Our society should be affected by our testimony and our conduct.

That is why Christians must possess each one of the Beatitudes. It is through them that they give flavor, influence the world, and manifest the high standard that God gives and expects of every true Christian. Only in this way will we show the lost people a better way, through the way we live; we will be able to lead them to Christ with our witness. Wherever the Christian has contact—in the family, at school, at work, in the neighborhood, whether it be in their private or public lives—they must carry these very outstanding features highlighted in the Beatitudes, which will positively and drastically influence society.

The living witness of the Beatitudes in us will enable the holy and just God of the Scriptures, with his eternal gospel, to be revealed to people. And this will make the light of Christ's salvation shine upon them.

The second quality of salt—especially in the days prior to refrigeration—is that it prevents the food from rotting. If you notice, even today this technique of salting the food is widely used for the same reason. When Christ compared us with salt, he wanted to teach that the portrayal of the Beatitudes in the life of the Christian acts to prevent the advance of sin, perversion, and corruption in the world.

This means that, wherever there is a faithful Christian, whether it is in society or in the home, their presence and their righteous and holy witness will inhibit sin. The presence of genuine Christians in a society will help prevent unjust laws from being approved, deter an escalation of sinfulness, or see that depravity does not prevail.

Just as salt works to keep food healthy, the Lord intended that those practicing the Beatitudes would work to preserve goodness, justice, holiness, and reverence. Therefore, the presence of a Christian in a given place must show these values. Their conduct should be such that they inhibit people from openly sinning, because there is a child of God in that place. It is the prerogative of blessed Christians to preserve the peace wherever they are, to maintain goodness, and to prevent godlessness from spreading.

For these reasons Jesus stated that Christians are the salt of the earth: they benefit all areas of society with their unique and peculiar flavor of preserving it from corruption.

For love of the Lord of glory, dear reader, you must strive to manifest each of the beatitudes daily: praying, studying the Scriptures, consecrating yourself, to live them out in their fullness, for only in this way will we be the ambassadors of King Jesus, pointing out to the lost world the path of reconciliation with God.

However, we do not stop here. In addition to the Beatitudes giving flavor and impeding the corruption of the world, they present a test of true conversion. Maybe you are not very sure about the authenticity of your conversion. Perhaps, dear reader, you have never made a careful self-examination of your spiritual life. You must carefully analyze yourself in light of the principles of the regenerated life portrayed in the Beatitudes, to attest to the genuineness of your salvation.

Are you poor in spirit? Do you weep for your sin and for the sin around you? Are you meek and humble of heart? Do you have hunger and thirst for the righteousness of God? Can you be considered pure in heart, someone in whom there is no willful misconduct? Are you a peacemaker? Do you suffer persecution for being a zealous imitator of Jesus Christ?

It is possible that after the study of the Beatitudes you have realized, with the help of the Holy Spirit, that there is no evidence of true salvation in your life. Perhaps your Christian life is a "façade," a complete illusion. It may be the fruit of a precipitated confession or emotional appeal to which you responded at some point in your life. It may be that there was no regeneration in your heart and your life was not transformed, giving you new character. Wouldn't that be the reason you have never manifested the Beatitudes?

Remember that they are fruits of true salvation, and if you have not experienced salvation in your life, the fruits that accompany it cannot be produced either. This book may be attesting that you have never been saved. I would like to urge you, dear reader, to acknowledge and confess your sin to the Lord. Repent with all of your heart. Humble yourself before the merciful Savior. Now seek Christ's salvation, pleading with him for a new heart.

Don't run away from your reality, even if it is extremely painful and too shocking. Look unto Christ, the Author and Finisher of the faith. Look at him on that bloody cross, taking away your sin, guilt, and condemnation. Contemplate him receiving in your place the wrath of God and dying as a perfect sacrifice so you could be justified. Remember, dear reader, that on the third day Jesus rose from the dead, thus giving the assurance that God accepted his sacrifice. He can forgive all sins and save all those who repent and deposit their faith in him, causing them to be received as children of God.

Cast all your hope on Christ, leaving aside any other form of salvation, whether through merit, effort, or works. Trust your salvation in the absolute, sufficient, and gracious work of Jesus on the cross of Calvary. By being saved by Christ you will gain eternal life. These characteristics, the Beatitudes, will then clothe you. You will finally be the salt of the earth and will influence this lost world as never before.

Finally, let us all, through the study of the Beatitudes, become better and mature Christians, in the likeness of the Son of God. May God, the Lord of Hosts, be exalted, honored, and receive all glory through our lives.

www.ingramcontent.com/pod-product-compliance
Lightning Source LLC
Chambersburg PA
CBHW070951180426
43194CB00042B/2247